Front Cover Design – eBook Version

How To Write Winning Letters of Recommendation
by Shaun Fawcett, M.B.A.

Eliminate Writer's Block Forever!

Instant Recommendation Letter Kit

Front Cover Design – eBook Version

INSTANT RECOMMENDATION LETTER KIT

HOW TO WRITE WINNING LETTERS OF RECOMMENDATION

By Shaun Fawcett, M.B.A.

"How To" Tips and Tricks
plus
35 Real-Life Downloadable Templates!

RECOMMENDATION LETTERS: employment, college…
REFERENCE LETTERS: employment, character, general…
COMMENDATION LETTERS: employment, community service…
PERFORMANCE EVALUATION LETTERS: college, university…
SPECIAL BONUS CHAPTER: COLLEGE ADMISSION ESSAYS

eBook Solutions.net
Saving You Time and Money

Copyright © 2002 by Shaun R. Fawcett

All rights reserved. No part of this book may be reproduced or transmitted in any form, by any means, without written permission from the author, except a reviewer, who may quote brief passages for a review.

National Library of Canada Cataloguing in Publication Data

Fawcett, Shaun, 1949-
Instant recommendation letter kit [electronic resource] : how to write winning letters of recommendation

Includes bibliographical references.

ISBN 0-9684297-5-0

1. Employment references. 2. Letter writing. I. Title.
HF5549.5.R45F38 2002   808'.06665   C2002-902875-2

Final Draft Publications
1501 Notre-Dame West, Suite No. 5
Montreal QC, Canada H3C 1L2

http://www.writinghelp-central.com

Disclaimer

This book was written as a guide only, and does not claim to be the final definitive word on any of the subjects covered. The statements made and opinions expressed are the personal observations and assessments of the author based on his own experiences and were not intended to prejudice any party. There may be errors or omissions in this guide. As such, the author or publisher does not accept any liability or responsibility for any loss or damage that may have been caused, or alleged to have been caused, through use of the information contained in this manual. Errors or omissions will be corrected in future editions, provided the publisher receives written notification of such.

TABLE OF CONTENTS

PREFACE TO SPECIAL PRINT EDITION 8

INTRODUCTION 10
BACKGROUND 10
WHAT THIS MANUAL COVERS 11
Recommendation Letters 11
Reference Letters 11
Commendation Letters 12
Performance Evaluation Letters 12
Writing College Admission Essays (BONUS!) 12
A DEFINITIVE WRITING RESOURCE 12
LETTER FORMATS USED IN THIS GUIDE 13

REAL-LIFE TEMPLATES FOR SUCCESS 14
"USE REAL-LIFE TEMPLATES FOR WRITING SUCCESS" 14
Fill-In-The-Blank Templates - Sample 14
Disadvantages Of Fill-In-The-Blank Templates 15
Real-Life Template - Sample 16
Advantages Of Real-Life Templates 17

RECOMMENDATION LETTERS DEFINED 19
"RECOMMENDATION LETTERS DEMYSTIFIED" 19
Letters Of Recommendation 20
Letters Of Reference 20
Commendation Letters 21
Performance Evaluation Letters 21

RECOMMENDATION LETTER GUIDELINES 23
"RECOMMENDATION LETTER TIPS AND STRATEGIES" 23
Write It Only If You Want To 23
If You Must Refuse, Do So Right Away 24
Suggest Someone Else 24
Write It As You See It 24
Be Honest, Fair, and Balanced 24

Balanced Is Best 25

LETTER WRITING GUIDELINES 26

"LETTER WRITING TIPS AND STRATEGIES" 26
Keep It Short And To The Point 26
Focus On The Recipient's Needs 27
Use Simple And Appropriate Language 27
Reread And Revise It 27
Check Spelling And Grammar 27

RECOMMENDATION LETTERS 29

EMPLOYMENT-RELATED RECOMMENDATION LETTERS 29

DRAFTING TIPS – EMPLOYMENT-RELATED LETTERS 30
Make Sure You're Comfortable 30
Define Background Parameters First 30
Ask For Input From The Requestor 30
Make Sure You Cover The Entire Person 30
Avoid Controversial Statements/Terminology 31
Use Active, Powerful Words 31
Review The Final Product 31

SAMPLE TEMPLATES - EMPLOYMENT RECOMMENDATION LETTERS 31
Recommendation Letter: Employment - Sample 1 (favorable) 32
Recommendation Letter: Employment - Sample 2 (balanced) 33
Recommendation Letter: Employment - Sample 3 (unfavorable) 34
Recommendation Letter: Employment - Sample 4 (targeted) 35
Recommendation Letter: Employment - Sample 5 (one project) 36
Recommendation Letter: Employment - Sample 6 (peer recommendation) ... 37
Recommendation Letter: Employment - Sample 7 (short-term project) 38
Recommendation Letter: Employment - Sample 8 (part-time student) 39
Recommendation Letter: Employment - Sample 9 (community service) ... 40
Recommendation Letter: Employment - Sample 10 (refusal to write one) . 41

COLLEGE-RELATED RECOMMENDATION LETTERS 42

DRAFTING TIPS – COLLEGE-RELATED RECOMMENDATION LETTERS 42
Make Sure You're The One 43
Allow Plenty of Lead-Time 43
Gather Background Information First 43
Write To A Specific Person 44
Get Input From The Requestor 44
Cover The Entire Person 44

- *Be Specific and Give Examples* 45
- *Avoid Controversial Statements/Terminology* 45
- *Use Active, Powerful Words* 45
- *Review The Final Product* 46

SAMPLE TEMPLATES - COLLEGE-RELATED RECOMMENDATION LETTERS 46
- *Recommendation Letter: College-Related - Sample 1 (undergraduate applicant)* 47
- *Recommendation Letter: College-Related - Sample 2 (mature student applicant)* 48
- *Recommendation Letter: College-Related - Sample 3 (undergraduate, first job)* 49
- *Recommendation Letter: College-Related - Sample 4 (graduate applicant)* 51
- *Recommendation Letter: College-Related - Sample 5 (scholarship applicant)* 53

REFERENCE LETTERS 55

DRAFTING TIPS – REFERENCE LETTERS 55
- *Make Sure You're The Right One* 56
- *Start With The Background Parameters* 56
- *Get Additional Input From Requestor* 57
- *Don't Get Too Specific* 57
- *Avoid Controversial Terminology* 57
- *Use Active, Powerful Words* 57
- *Review The Final Product* 58

SAMPLE TEMPLATES - REFERENCE LETTERS 58
- *Reference Letter: Sample 1 (employment)* 59
- *Reference Letter: Sample 2 (character, friend)* 60
- *Reference Letter: Sample 3 (character, general)* 61
- *Reference Letter: Sample 4 (former customer)* 62
- *Reference Letter: Sample 5 (explain departure)* 63

COMMENDATION LETTERS 64

DRAFTING TIPS – COMMENDATION LETTERS 64
- *Think About It Carefully* 64
- *Do Some Basic Checking* 65
- *Get Proper Background Information* 65
- *Brace Yourself For Repercussions* 66

SAMPLE TEMPLATES - COMMENDATION LETTERS 66
- *Commendation Letter: Sample 1 (corporate)* 67
- *Commendation Letter: Sample 2 (customer service)* 68
- *Commendation Letter: Sample 3 (teacher)* 69
- *Commendation Letter: Sample 4 (award)* 70
- *Commendation Letter: Sample 5 (community service)* 71

PERFORMANCE EVALUATION LETTERS 72

DRAFTING TIPS – EVALUATION LETTERS 72
Stick To The Facts 72
Try To Keep It Short 73
Watch Your Language 73
Keep It Confidential 73

SAMPLE TEMPLATES - EVALUATION LETTERS 74
Evaluation Letter: Sample 1 (satisfactory) 75
Evaluation Letter: Sample 2 (excellent) 77
Evaluation Letter: Sample 3 (borderline) 80
Evaluation Letter: Sample 4 (unsatisfactory) 83
Evaluation Letter: Sample 5 (request for letter) 85

BONUS SECTION!

COLLEGE ADMISSION ESSAYS 86

ADMISSION ESSAY TERMINOLOGY AND REQUIREMENTS 86
ADMISSION ESSAY REVIEW PROCESS 87
WHAT THEY'RE LOOKING FOR 88
DRAFTING TIPS – COLLEGE ADMISSION ESSAYS 89
Make It A Personal Statement 89
Write It For The Committee 89
Keep The Language and Structure Simple 90
Don't Repeat What They Already Know 90
Answer The Question 90
Don't Try To Be Too Cute 91
Target The School If Possible 91
Focus On Your Uniqueness 92
Tell A Story Of Personal Change and Growth 92
Write About You and What You Know 93
Avoid Controversial Subjects 93
Provide Supporting Details 93
Draft and Then Re-Draft 94
Proof Read and Edit Carefully 94
Get Feedback From Others 95
Sleep On It One More Time 95

SAMPLE TEMPLATES – COLLEGE ADMISSION ESSAYS 95
Admission Essay: Sample 1 (life-changing experiences) 97

Admission Essay: Sample 2 (travel and cultural diversity).. 99
Admission Essay: Sample 3 (targeted university) 101
Admission Essay: Sample 4 (career and personal goals) 103
Admission Essay: Sample 5 (social issues and concerns).. 105
COMMERCIAL WRITING SERVICES – COLLEGE ADMISSION ESSAYS 107

ONLINE RESOURCE LINKS 108

HOW-TO INFORMATION LINKS 108
EMPLOYMENT-RELATED SITES 110
COLLEGE-RELATED SITES – TIPS AND SAMPLES 110
COLLEGE-RELATED SITES - RECOMMENDATION LETTER FORMS 112
RECOMMENDATION LETTER SERVICES 113
COLLEGE ADMISSION ESSAY LINKS 114

Special Note Re: Hyperlinks

Because this book was first published as an eBook with "live" clickable hyperlinks throughout, those links have also been displayed in this printed version for your information. Even though these links are not clickable in this book they still provide the pertinent Web site URL address that you can type into your Internet browser should you want to explore online for further information.

In addition, you can request that a copy of the templates be e-mailed to you as per the instructions in the following Special Preface section. That templates document also includes live clickable links for all of the links included on pages 105 to 112 of this book (MS-Word document).

PREFACE TO SPECIAL PRINT EDITION

Instant Recommendation Letter Kit was initially conceived and written as an online eBook. Since late July 2002 the eBook version has been available to purchase online from a dedicated Web site:

http://www.instantrecommendationletterkit.com

From the moment that Web site went "live" online, the eBook has sold very well because it fills an important information gap for many people.

Nevertheless, I realized from the beginning that no matter how much I publicized that eBook Web site, many people in need of recommendation letter help and information would never become aware of it. So I decided to try alternative distribution channels, offline.

Consequently, this version of the eBook is a special one that is being made available through some of the more traditional printed book marketing channels. So if you are reading this, it should be because you purchased the eBook in hard copy form through a large traditional book distribution company such as amazon.com, Ingram, or others.

Get Your Downloadable Templates

There is one key difference between this print book that you purchased through a distributor and what you would have received had you purchased and downloaded the eBook from my Web site.

With the Web site purchase you can download the Bonus Templates (MS-Word format) straight to your computer at the time of purchase. For technical reasons, that was not possible with a printed book when going through a standard distributor.

Nevertheless, since the templates are an integral part of the Kit, I wanted to make sure that you have access to them. **To receive your Free copy of the Bonus Templates file, please send an e-mail to the following address:**

mailto:templates@instantrecommendationletterkit.com

In that e-mail you MUST include the following information: your full name, full telephone number, your primary e-mail address, and the date of purchase. Also indicate which business from which you purchased the Kit, and include the Order Number or Transaction Number you were given at the time of purchase.

Once we have received your e-mail and verified your purchase, we will send you the Bonus Templates as an e-mail attachment to the address you specify. You should receive it within a few hours of making your request, 24 hours at the most.

This eBook Has Two Parts

When this book is sold from my Web site it comes in three downloadable parts: 1. The Main Writing Kit (pdf), 2. The Bonus Templates (MS-Word), 3. The Bonus Buyer's Guide (pdf).

As explained above, for technical reasons, this special printed version of the Kit has been packaged slightly differently. This printed version of the book is divided into two parts as follows:

1. **Instant Recommendation Letter Kit (113 page pdf eBook)**

2. **Bonus Buyers Guide (44 page pdf eBook)**

In total, you get a two-part book of 164 pages. As explained on the previous page, the downloadable Bonus Templates are not included with the eBook but may be ordered for Free by e-mail at the address given.

Remember, when requesting your downloadable Bonus Templates make sure that you include the following information in your e-mail: your full name, full telephone number, your primary e-mail address, and the date of purchase. Also indicate which business you purchased the Kit from, and include the Order Number or Transaction Number you were given at the time of purchase.

mailto:templates@instantrecommendationletterkit.com

INTRODUCTION

BACKGROUND

This is the second in a series of practical "writing kits" based on the use of downloadable real-life sample templates.

The first in the series was *Instant Home Writing Kit*, which was initially published in September 2001. That Kit covers a broad range of writing-related subjects including: letter writing, resume writing, report writing, APA and MLA writing styles, e-mails, business reports, etc.

That Writing Kit also contains more than 60 fully-formatted real-life templates that users can download straight into their word processing program and work with as they choose.

If you aren't familiar with Instant Home Writing Kit, you can check it out at: http://www.instanthomewritingkit.com

Instant Recommendation Letter Kit is much more focused than its predecessor. It concentrates on the development and writing of the various types of "letters of recommendation" that are most widely used, namely:

- recommendation letters (letters of recommendation)
- reference letters (letters of reference)
- commendation letters (letters of commendation)
- performance evaluation letters (letters of evaluation, evaluation letters)

The idea for this particular e-Book grew directly out of visitor reaction to my Web site at: http://www.writinghelp-central.com.

After monitoring visitors to that Web site during its first year of operation, it became clear that a large majority of people arrived there looking for letter-writing information and samples specifically related to the keywords "letter of recommendation" and "recommendation letter."

As a result, I concluded that there was a definite need for a practical quick reference "recommendation letter kit" with "real-life" sample templates.

Accordingly, *Instant Recommendation Letter Kit* was born. It has been designed as a quick-reference home and home-business writing guide, focused on simplifying the often difficult and delicate task of writing the various types of letters of recommendation.

But most importantly, *Instant Recommendation Letter Kit* is a practical hands-on "toolkit" that people can use whenever they have to write a recommendation letter of any kind.

Using the "real-life templates" included with the Kit, you will never again have to start a letter of recommendation from a blank page or screen. You can work directly from the real-life templates that you can download straight into your word-processing program. (MS-Word compatible).

If you ever need to write any type of letter of recommendation, this Kit will definitely simplify your life.

WHAT THIS MANUAL COVERS

This manual covers all known types of letters of recommendation. These letters are most often employment-related or education-related. Following is a list of the most common types of letters that fall into the broad "letters of reference" category.

Recommendation Letters

Also known as letters of recommendation, the majority of recommendation letters are related to employment situations, and admission to college and graduate school.

Reference Letters

Often confused with their closely-related cousins recommendation letters, letters of reference are usually employment-related and character-related.

Commendation Letters

Letters of commendation are most often written in work-related or community service situations.

Performance Evaluation Letters

Performance evaluation letters are usually written in employment and school related situations.

This manual offers valuable tips, tricks and information to help you with the development and writing of just about any kind of letter of recommendation.

In addition, this guide contains "real-life templates" as samples of the various letters presented. The value and advantages of "real-life templates" are explained in the following section.

Writing College Admission Essays (BONUS!)

In addition to the various types of letters of recommendation a 20-page **Bonus Chapter** has also been included on how to write an admission essay for college or university. If one needs a recommendation letter for college or university, one will also need to know how to write admission essays.

This bonus chapter includes five (5) fully-formatted real-life college admission essays that you can download and adapt to your situation.

A DEFINITIVE WRITING RESOURCE

While researching this topic I was amazed to discover all of the confusion surrounding the seemingly simple term "recommendation letter". I was even more amazed when I started looking around for a definitive and complete resource book on the recommendation letter in all of its various forms.

As far as I know, a complete guide to writing all types of recommendation letters does not exist. (Until this one came along, of course!).

When I discovered that, I set out to make this THE complete and definitive guide on ALL types of recommendation letters.

I believe I have succeeded in that task. Anyone needing to write any type of "recommendation letter" will find what they need somewhere in this guide.

However, nobody is perfect. If you find a true recommendation letter application that is not covered in this guide, please let me know and I will make sure that the next version includes it. Just drop me a quick e-mail at:

mailto:www.instantrecommendationletterkit.com

LETTER FORMATS USED IN THIS GUIDE

Most of the sample letters and templates included in this Kit are business letters of one description or another. There are many possible formats or page layouts for business letters.

Depending on which letter writing text you reference, the number, and names of the various formats will differ. There seems to be no general international standard to use for writing business letters.

Consequently, I have decided to use my personal favorite letter format in all of the templates/samples throughout this document. It's called the ***Modified Semi-Block Style***. Essentially, it places all major blocks flush to the left-hand margin, except for the date and return address blocks at the top of the letter, which are placed flush to the right margin. (see sample letters).

If you are interested, the following link will give you the specifics on some of the other possible business letter formats available:

http://jobsearchtech.about.com/library/bl-business-letter-samples.htm

Most large organizations have a "corporate style manual" that specifies the standard formats for letters at that particular organization.

The main thing is to choose one style that you like and stick with it.

Now, let's get into the heart of this manual and find out what real life recommendation letters are all about.

REAL-LIFE TEMPLATES FOR SUCCESS

The sample templates for all of the various types of letters of recommendation contained in this Kit are in a format that I call "fully-formatted real-life templates".

I am convinced that real-life templates are by far the most useful to people when they need to draft a letter of recommendation on their own. These templates are a quantum leap beyond the traditional "fill-in-the-blank" templates.

The rest of this section is an expanded version of an article I wrote in early 2002 entitled *"Use Real-Life Templates For Writing Success"*. That original article was published in various eZines and posted on various Web sites across the Internet.

"USE REAL-LIFE TEMPLATES FOR WRITING SUCCESS"

At some point along the way, most of us have used what are commonly called "fill-in-the-blank" writing templates. We might have used them to write a letter, format an essay, or set-up a resume or c.v.

You know what I'm talking about here. It's those form letter templates that you see in many writing texts and workbooks.

Fill-In-The-Blank Templates - Sample

For example, in the case of a letter, a "fill-in-the-blank" template would look something like this:

> Dear [NAME OF RECIPIENT]:
>
> This is to advise you that your probation period in the position [POSITION NAME] expired on [DATE].

> The [NAME OF REVIEW COMMITTEE] met on [DATE OF MEETING] and determined that your probationary appointment was successful and that you should be immediately appointed to [NAME OF POSITION] [NAME OF ORGANIZATIONAL UNIT].
>
> Accordingly, this is to inform you that effective [DATE OF APPOINTMENT] you are officially appointed to the position of [NAME OF POSITION] for an initial period of [NUMBER OF YEARS/MONTHS]. Terms and conditions of your employment are
> covered by [OFFICIAL CONTRACT NAME/NUMBER].
>
> Would you please report as soon as possible to [NAME OF OFFICIAL], [TITLE OF OFFICIAL] in the [OFFICIAL NAME OF HR GROUP] so that the details of your appointment may be properly documented.
>
> Congratulations [NAME OF APPOINTEE]. All of us at [COMPANY OR ORGANIZATION NAME] look forward to working with you in
> the future.
>
> Sincerely,
>
> [NAME OF ORIGINATOR]
> [TITLE OF ORIGINATOR]

Although this "fill-in-the-blank" approach can work, it has a number of shortcomings as follows:

Disadvantages Of Fill-In-The-Blank Templates

- Because of their generic nature, they tend to generalize so much that they resemble a computer-generated form letter.

- They don't provide specific information on how a professional would properly fill in the required information [THE BLANKS].

- The content is typically watered-down using generic terms in order to try and cover every possible situation.

- They don't provide mental stimulation or show how a professional might word the letter in a specific real-life context.

- They are difficult to work with and virtually useless for 98% of real-life situations, since they lack real-life content.

Real-Life Template - Sample

On the other hand, here's what a "real-life template" would look like for the same situation covered above:

Dear Jessica:

This is to advise you that your probation period in the position Customer Service Agent (Temporary) expired on November 30, 2002.

The Staffing Review Committee met late last week and determined that your probationary appointment was successful and that you should be appointed immediately as Customer Service Agent (Ongoing).

Accordingly, this is to inform you that effective December 1, 2002, you are officially appointed to the position of Customer Service Agent in the Customer Support Group. The initial appointment will be for a period of 36 months. Terms and conditions of your employment are covered by the Customer Service Group Employment Agreement.

Would you please report as soon as possible to Jim Jackson, Chief of Human Resources so that the details of your appointment may be properly documented.

Congratulations Jessica! All of us here at MedWay Systems Inc. look forward to continuing to work with you in the future.

Sincerely,

Sharon Smithson
Manager, Customer Support Group

Advantages Of Real-Life Templates

Clearly, there can be no doubt that the "model" that most of us would rather work with, if we had to write a similar letter, is definitely the second one, the "real-life" template.

Why is that?

It's because you can relate to it. It talks about real-life people in a real-life situation that you can identify with. And, you get to see exactly how a professional writer worded it in a particular context.

Here are the main advantages of "real-life" templates.

Content With Value

It is much easier to adapt "real-life" templates to YOUR actual situations because they give you visual and intellectual cues to which you can relate.

Naturally, when you see how a copywriter or consultant has dealt with a "real-life" scenario, in terms of word choice, context, and punctuation, it is much easier to adapt to the real-life situation that you are writing for. In that way, the actual content has value.

Easy To Work With

"Real-life" templates are just as easy to work with as the other templates. You simply load them into your word processing program and edit and adjust them to fit your own specific situation. Presto! You have a fully formatted real-life letter ready to be printed and sent out in the mail.

You also have the comfort of knowing that what you are sending has already been used in other "real-life" situations.

Real-Life Content

With real-life templates, it is much easier to find an adaptable "fit" for the situation you are writing for. Not only do they give you the final format of a document, their content provides an excellent real-life sample and gives food-for-thought to assist you in the writing process.
document, their content provides an excellent real-life sample and gives food-for-thought to assist you in the writing process.

Fully-Formatted Final Versions

"Real-life" templates are fully-formatted as final documents so that you can see exactly what they looked like when they were sent out in "real-life" situations. They don't look like some kind of "draft" computer-generated form letter.

Go ahead. Browse through the sample letter templates found later in this Kit.

Are you back yet? Ok.

Now I ask you, would you rather work from a "fill-in-the-blanks" generic template or a fully-formatted "real-life" template?

I have no doubt that the vast majority of readers would choose the latter for all of the reasons given earlier.

Reality Check

All of the sample templates presented in this Kit are based on real-life situations using real-life content, for all of the reasons described above.

However, names, addresses, phone numbers, etc. that could be used to specifically identify an individual have been altered to protect privacy.

Downloadable Templates

As explained in the Special Preface of this book (pages 8 and 9), the downloadable Bonus Templates (M-Word format) may be ordered for Free by e-mail at the address given below.

Remember, when requesting your downloadable Bonus Templates make sure that you include the following information: your full name, full telephone number, your primary e-mail address, and the date of purchase. Also indicate which business from which you purchased the Kit, and include the Order or Transaction Number you were given at the time of purchase.

mailto:templates@instantrecommendationletterkit.com

RECOMMENDATION LETTERS DEFINED

Information about letters of recommendation and sample recommendation letters are by far the most often clicked letter-related links at my *www.writinghelp-central.com*. Web site.

Typically, a recommendation letter conveys one person's view of the working performance and general workplace demeanor of a person who has worked under their direct supervision.

Recommendation letters are generally requested when the requestor is applying for a new job, or when they are trying to get accepted into a college or university program.

Of course, the usual expectation is that a recommendation or reference letter will be positive overall.

This section contains an expanded version of an article I wrote in early 2002 entitled *"Recommendation Letters Demystified"*. That article was published in selected e-Zines and posted on various Web sites across the Internet.

"RECOMMENDATION LETTERS DEMYSTIFIED"

There is a lot of confusion about recommendation letters.

Recommendation letters are often referred to in a number of different ways including: letters of recommendation, reference letters, letters of reference, commendation letters, and sometimes even, performance evaluation letters.

This terminology can be quite confusing, especially when these terms are often used interchangeably, sometimes to mean the same thing, sometimes to mean something different.

Below are some definitions that should clear up any confusion, followed by some tips and strategies on how best to deal with recommendation letters.

Letters Of Recommendation

Employment-Related

Also called a recommendation letter, it is an employment-related letter that is specifically requested by the person the letter is being written about. Such a letter is normally positive in nature, and written by someone who knows the subject well enough to comment on the skills, abilities, and specific work attributes of that person.

Typically, an employment-related recommendation letter conveys one person's view of the work performance and general workplace demeanor of another person that has worked under their direct supervision. The requestor of the letter normally requests such a letter to use when applying for a promotion or a new job.

These letters are usually addressed to a specific person to whom the requestor has been asked to submit the letter.

College- and University-Related

Another situation where recommendation letters are a common requirement is for entry into undergraduate and graduate programs at a college or university. Graduate programs often require two or more letters of recommendation as part of the program admission requirements.

Normally, these college-related recommendation letters are written at the request of the program applicant by people who know them and are familiar with their academic career to date, and their future education and career aspirations. These people could include: former teachers, community leaders, school faculty members, administrators, academic supervisors, and/or employers.

These letters are always addressed to a specific person and are normally included as part of the program admission application.

Letters Of Reference

These are more general letters that are often requested by employees when they leave the employ of an organization. Normally factual in nature, they are usually addressed, "to whom it may concern" and provide basic information such as: work history, dates of employment, positions held, academic credentials, etc.

Reference letters sometimes contain a general statement (as long as a positive one can be made), about the employee's work record with the company that they are leaving. Employees often submit these letters with job applications in the hope that the letter will reflect favorably on their chances for the new position.

Character reference letters are sometimes required by employers when hiring individuals to perform personal or residential services such as child care, domestic services, etc. These letters are usually drafted by a former employer and deal with such characteristics as honesty, dependability and work ethic/performance.

Commendation Letters

These are usually unsolicited letters, which typically commend an employee to their supervisor for something outstanding or noteworthy that the employee has done. Usually, the employee would have to do something "above and beyond" what is normally expected of them in their job to warrant such a letter.

Typically, these letters are written by co-workers, or managers from another area of the organization who were suitably impressed while supervising the person on a short-term project.

Commendation letters are also used to nominate individuals for special awards of recognition for outstanding public service.

Performance Evaluation Letters

These are usually detailed assessments of an employee's work performance as part of an organization's regular employee review process. Typically, they are written by the employee's supervisor and are attached to the individual's performance appraisal and placed in their personnel file.

The format and structure for this type of letter is more often than not dictated by the employee performance evaluation system or process that is in-place wherever the subject of the letter is employed.

However, in the academic environment in North America there is often a requirement for a specific "performance evaluation letter" for the assessment of academic staff. A number of real-life templates of academic-related performance evaluation letters are included in the appropriate section of this guide.

In addition, the Online Resources Links chapter at the end of this guide contains link to various types of performance evaluation letters, from both the academic sector and other employment sectors.

RECOMMENDATION LETTER GUIDELINES

In addition to standard letter-writing protocol, there are a number of basic guidelines that cover most situations related to the writing of recommendation letters specifically. These are usually more "situational" than "how to" in nature.

The "how tos" of writing recommendation letters are covered a bit later on in the section titled "Letter Writing Guidelines".

These recommendation letter guidelines are important to both note and apply, since writing letters of recommendation is always a somewhat tricky and delicate matter. This is because they almost always affect the reputation and future of another person.

The following is another excerpt from an article I wrote in early 2002 entitled *"Recommendation Letters Demystified."* That article was published in numerous e-Zines and posted on various Web sites across the Internet.

"RECOMMENDATION LETTER TIPS AND STRATEGIES"

The following tips apply primarily to the writing of recommendation letters and reference letters as defined above.

Write It Only If You Want To

If you are asked by someone to write a letter of recommendation about them, you don't have to say "yes" automatically. If it is someone you respect for their work, and you have mostly positive things to say about them, by all means write the letter.

There is no point saying "yes" and then writing a letter that says nothing good about the person, or worse still, concocting a misleading positive assessment of someone.

If You Must Refuse, Do So Right Away

On the other hand, if someone asks you to write a letter of reference for them, and you know you will be hard-pressed to keep the overall letter positive, say "no" right up front. No point in hesitating and leading them on to believe that the answer might be "yes".

A gentle but firm "no" will usually get the message across to the person. Explain that you don't think that you are the best (or most qualified) person to do it.

Suggest Someone Else

If you feel you should refuse, for whatever reason, it may be helpful for you to suggest someone else who you think might have a more positive and/or accurate assessment of the person. That person may also be in a better position to do the assessment. Usually there are a number of possible candidates, and you may not actually be the best person.

In fact, I have seen a number of cases over the years where people requesting recommendation letters have not requested the letter from the obvious or logical choice. They usually do this when they don't like the obvious choice or are worried about what that person will say about them.

Write It As You See It

Writing a less than honest recommendation letter does no one a favor in the end. It is likely to backfire on you, the person being recommended, and the new employer.

Also, many employers and head-hunting agencies check references. How would you like to be called up and have to mislead people due to questionable things you may have written in a reference letter?

Be Honest, Fair, and Balanced

Honesty is always the best policy when it comes to writing recommendation letters. At the same time, try to be fair and balanced in your approach.

If in your estimation, a person has five strengths and one glaring weakness, but that weakness really bothers you, make sure you don't over-emphasize the weak point in the letter, based on your personal bias. Just mention it as a weakness and move on.

Balanced Is Best

An overall balanced approach is the best one for a letter of recommendation. Even if your letter generally raves about how excellent the person is, some balance on the other side of the ledger will make it more credible. After all, nobody's perfect.

There must be some area where the person being recommended needs to improve. A bit of constructive criticism never hurts.

LETTER WRITING GUIDELINES

Even though this guide is written specifically to cover the writing of letters of recommendation, many of the basic principles of letter writing in general still apply and should be observed.

This section provides a brief review of the most important guidelines to follow when writing letters in general, and thus by definition recommendation letters as well

Based on the feedback that I have been getting from visitors to the **writinghelp-central.com** site, general letter writing is definitely the area where most people are looking for help or guidance.

In fact, over 55% of the visitors to my site are seeking some sort of letter writing information or assistance. And, as I stated earlier, the vast majority of them are looking for information related to recommendation letters.

The following is a slightly expanded version of an article I wrote in early 2002 entitled *"7 Essential Letter-Writing Strategies"*. That article was published in numerous eZines and posted on various Web sites.

"LETTER WRITING TIPS AND STRATEGIES"

Here are a few practical letter writing tips adapted from the **writinghelp-central.com** Web site to help you when writing that next letter:

Keep It Short And To The Point

Letters involving business (both personal or corporate) should be concise, factual, and focused. Try to never exceed one page or you will be in risk of losing your reader. A typical letter page will hold 350 to 400 words.

If you can't get your point across with that many words you probably haven't done enough preparatory work. If necessary, call the recipient on the phone to clarify any fuzzy points and then use the letter just to summarize the overall situation.

Focus On The Recipient's Needs

While writing the letter, focus on the information requirements of your audience, the intended addressee. If you can, in your "mind's eye" imagine the intended recipient seated across a desk or boardroom table from you while you are explaining the subject of the letter.

What essential information does that person need to know through this communication? What will be their expectations when they open the letter? Have these all been addressed?

Use Simple And Appropriate Language

For clarity and precision, your letter should use simple straightforward language. Use short sentences and don't let paragraphs exceed three or four sentences. As much as possible, use language and terminology familiar to the intended recipient.

Don't use technical terms and acronyms without explaining them, unless you're certain the addressee is familiar with them.

Reread And Revise It

Do a first draft, and then carefully review and revise it. Put yourself in the place of the addressee. Imagine yourself receiving the letter. How would you react to it? Would it answer all of your questions? Does it deal with all of the key issues? Are the language and tone appropriate?

Sometimes reading it out loud to one's self can help. When you actually "hear" the words it is easy to tell if it "sounds" right, or not. I do this all the time and it really works.

Check Spelling And Grammar

A letter is a direct reflection of the person sending it, and by extension, the organization that person works for. When the final content of the letter is settled, make sure that you run it through a spelling and grammar checker. To send a letter with obvious spelling and grammatical errors is sloppy and unprofessional. In such cases, the recipient can't really be blamed for seeing this as an indication as to how you (and/or your organization) probably do most other things.

Spell-checkers are great, but they don't catch everything. For example, I often reverse the letters in certain words when typing quickly. i.e. "form" instead of "from." As far as a spell-checker is concerned, these are both valid words. Some grammar checkers will flag this as being out of context, but you can't always count on that.

The only way to be sure in the end that everything is fine, is to have someone with good spelling and grammar skills do a final check.

The above basic letter writing tips are mostly common sense. Nevertheless, **you would be amazed** how often these very basic "rules of thumb" are not employed when people are writing letters.

RECOMMENDATION LETTERS

As mentioned previously, there is often a lot of confusion as to what constitutes a real recommendation letter.

Recommendation letters are often referred to in a number of different ways including: letters of recommendation, reference letters, letters of reference, commendation letters, and sometimes even, performance evaluation letters.

This terminology can be quite confusing, especially when these terms are often used interchangeably, sometimes to mean the same thing, sometimes to mean something different.

So, to be absolutely clear, **in this section** we are referring specifically to the recommendation letters (i.e. letters of recommendation) that are either **employment-related or college-related.**

The following pages define and summarize the characteristics of these types of recommendation letters and provide sample templates for various real-life situations.

EMPLOYMENT-RELATED RECOMMENDATION LETTERS

An employment-related recommendation letter is one that is specifically requested by the person the letter is being written about. Such a letter is normally positive in nature, and written by someone who knows the subject well enough to comment on the skills, abilities, and specific work attributes of that person.

Typically, an employment-related recommendation letter conveys one person's view of the work performance and general workplace demeanor of a person who has worked under their direct supervision. The requestor of the letter normally requires it when applying for a promotion or a new job.

These letters are usually addressed to a specific person to whom the requestor has been asked to submit the letter.

Drafting Tips – Employment-Related Letters

If you are asked by someone to write a letter of recommendation for them, here are a few important points to keep in mind:

Make Sure You're Comfortable

If you feel that you don't know the person well enough you should decline, stating that as your reason. Also, you may find that it would be difficult for you to say very much positive about the person requesting the letter. However, if you are the requestor's direct supervisor (or former supervisor) you really don't have a choice, but you will have to be honest. Fair, too!

Define Background Parameters First

Before starting to write, make sure you know exactly to whom you are writing. Knowing the name and specific position of the addressee will help the mental process while drafting the letter. In the opening paragraph provide all of the background information such as: relationship to the person, organization, position titles, and time-frame and dates covered by your assessment, and other relevant overall background information.

Ask For Input From The Requestor

If you feel you need more information, don't hesitate to ask the requestor for a copy of their resume/cv. In addition, if you have access to them, you may want to have a quick review of recent performance evaluations. Finally, you can ask the requestor to jot down some key points they would like you to mention (at your discretion). This would include such things as highlighting their work and accomplishments on a special project or task force, etc.

Make Sure You Cover The Entire Person

Your letter should address all of the areas of the person that are job performance related. This would include such things as: basic job performance, motivation level, communication abilities, flexibility, adaptability, energy level, quality of outputs, initiative, leadership, goals achievement success, teamwork, etc. Always try to give a specific example rather than just making an open-ended generalization.

For example, "Shirley's exemplary performance as a Task Force Team Leader in the Restructuring Project highlighted her superior leadership and communication abilities" rather than, "Shirley has superior leadership and communication skills."

Avoid Controversial Statements/Terminology

Do not make statements that you cannot clearly support with facts. For example, statements such as "I believe Frank displays this tendency because he is the product of a dysfunctional background" are clearly not acceptable. Make sure you avoid using any words or terminology that could be deemed discriminatory such as: race, color, religion, political affiliation, sex, sexual orientation, age, physical appearance, handicaps, marital status, etc.

Use Active, Powerful Words

Neutral words such as good, nice, satisfactory, fair, reasonable, etc. should be avoided. Use active, descriptive words and terms such as: intelligent, assertive, initiator, self-starter, motivated, hard-working, cooperative, productive, creative, articulate, leader, communicator, team player, innovative, effective, efficient, honest, dependable, mature, etc.

Review The Final Product

Before signing your letter, do a final careful review. Check all spelling and grammar and make sure the terminology used is appropriate. Read it out loud to yourself and imagine being the recipient. Is it fair and balanced? Does it truly convey what you believe and want to say about the person who you are recommending? If not, revise it.

SAMPLE TEMPLATES - EMPLOYMENT RECOMMENDATION LETTERS

The following pages contain ten (10) real-life templates of employment-related recommendation letters for various situations.

Recommendation Letter: Employment - Sample 1 (favorable)

(print a Recommendation Letter on company letterhead paper)

July 30, 2002

Mr. Rodney Sims
Director, Marketing Services
Newport Industries Inc.
1500 Elm St.
Dallas, TX 75270

RE: Employment Recommendation – Maria Fuentas

Dear Rodney Sims:

This is in response to your recent request for a letter of recommendation for Maria Fuentas who worked for me up until two years ago.

Maria Fuentas worked under my direct supervision at Jasminder Technologies for a period of five years, ending in May 2000. During that period, I had the great pleasure of seeing her blossom from a junior marketing trainee at the beginning, into a fully functioning Marketing Program Co-Ordinator in her final two years with the company. This was the last position she held before moving on to a better career opportunity elsewhere.

Maria is a hard-working self-starter who invariably understands exactly what a project is all about from the outset, and how to get it done quickly and effectively. During her two years in the Marketing Co-Ordinator position, I cannot remember an instance in which she missed a major deadline. She often brought projects in below budget and ahead of schedule.

Ms. Fuentas is a resourceful, creative, and solution-oriented person who was frequently able to come up with new and innovative approaches to her assigned projects. She functioned well as a team leader when required, and she worked effectively as a team member under the direction of other team leaders.

On the interpersonal side, Maria has superior written and verbal communication skills. She gets along extremely well with staff under her supervision, as well as colleagues at her own level. She is highly respected, as both a person and a professional, by colleagues, employees, suppliers, and customers alike.

Two years ago, when Ms. Fuentas announced her resignation to take up a new position with a larger company, we were saddened to see her leave, although we wished her the greatest success in her new undertaking. Even now, two years after her departure, I can state that her presence, both as a person and as an exemplary employee, is still missed here.

In closing, as detailed above, based on my experience working with her, I can unreservedly recommend Maria Fuentas to you for any intermediate to senior marketing support position. If you would like further elaboration, feel free to call me at (416) 765-4293.

Sincerely,

Robert Christie
Director, Marketing and Sales

Recommendation Letter: Employment - Sample 2 (balanced)

(print a Recommendation Letter on company letterhead paper)

June 28, 2002

Mr. Stewart Hamilton
Project General Manager
Airport Expansion Project
Grantley Adams Int'l Airport
Christchurch, Barbados, West Indies

Dear Stewart Hamilton:

I am writing this letter at the request of David Handridge who has recently applied for the position of Graphic Design Supervisor on your project.

David worked under my direct supervision in the position of project team Graphic Artist and Designer for a three-year period in the late 1990's. Overall, I would say that he was an excellent employee who fulfilled the duties of his position in an exemplary way.

As an artist and designer, David was first rate, consistently producing high quality work in a timely fashion. When creative work was required, his work was always innovative and fresh. On the technical and engineering side he also produced good accurate work, even though he much preferred the creative assignments. I think it is fair to say that David never let his creative passion get in the way of his technical obligation.

The only area of weakness that I ever noted in David's performance was in his supervisory skills. In his position with the project team he had two junior artists reporting to him. In addition, he was occasionally called upon to supervise contracted graphic artists on larger rush projects.

The problem that came up on a number of occasions was David's inability or reluctance to fully delegate work to his staff. We discussed this issue a number of times and our conclusion was that, David being a perfectionist by nature, felt he had to have a direct hand in all of the work of his subordinates, no matter how routine. Needless to say, on occasion this tendency did cause some problems with staff and had some repercussions on meeting overall project deadlines.

When David approached me about writing this letter, we did discuss this one area of weakness. He now assures me that, in the three years since we worked together, he has completely overcome this one shortcoming through a combination of training and ongoing practical experience.

This being the case, I have no hesitation in recommending David Handridge to you for the position of Graphics Design Supervisor on your team.

I should add that, on the interpersonal side, David is a wonderful person and a good communicator who gets along with people very well, even under heavy deadline pressures.

Should you require further elaboration, don't hesitate to contact me at (416) 742-1594.

Sincerely,

Roger Neilson, CMA
Partner, ADN Engineering Systems Inc.

Recommendation Letter: Employment - Sample 3 (unfavorable)

(print a Recommendation Letter from a private citizen on regular stationery)

532 Drummond St.
Perth, ON
K7H 4N5

November 20, 2002

Ms. Jean Rogers
Chairperson
Adult Programs - Community
 Consultation and Advisory Committee
War Memorial Hospital
Perth, ON, K7N 4R2

<u>CONFIDENTIAL</u>

Dear Jean Rogers:

This is in reply to your recent letter to me in which you asked my opinion of Mr. Robert Jackman as a possible member of your Advisory Committee.

Based on your letter, it is my clear understanding that you have contacted me on this in complete confidence, because I previously held the position of Chairperson of your committee. On that strictly confidential basis, I have the following comments to make about Mr. Jackman as they relate to him as a possible candidate for your committee.

I have known Robert Jackman for more than 25 years, nine of which we worked together as insurance underwriters for the Mutual-Benefit Insurance Group. During that 25-year period Mr. Carson and I also served on a number of local community committees together.

Although I respect Mr. Jackman as a highly successful insurance underwriter, I must say in all honesty that I cannot recommend him for service on your committee. Without resorting to personal assassination, I have to state that Mr. Jackman can be very difficult to work with at times, especially in a committee situation. He seems to have a strong need to always be in charge, whether he is chairperson or not. He often tends to be autocratic and obstinate, and is almost invariably in disagreement with the vast majority of his colleagues.

You may recall two years ago when the Parks and Monuments Committee resigned en masse. That unfortunate group resignation was a direct result of Mr. Jackman, who was chairperson at the time, unilaterally making unpopular decisions without consulting with his committee members. This is just one example of the kind of problems Mr. Jackman has caused over the years. There are numerous others, which I won't go into here.

In closing, based on my experience working with Robert Jackman, both professionally and in community service over a 25-year period, I cannot in good conscience recommend him to you for appointment to your advisory committee.

If you have any questions on this, please don't hesitate to call me at 371-5289.

Sincerely,

Randolf Smithfield

Recommendation Letter: Employment - Sample 4 (targeted)

(print a Recommendation Letter on company letterhead paper)

August 31, 2002

Ms. Helena Nearington
Executive Editor, Corporate
Griffon Communications Inc.
122 Sixth Avenue,
New York, NY 10011
(212) 632-1789

Dear Ms. Nearington:

Jeremy Cook requested that I write this letter to you with reference to his recent application to your company as a Senior Graphics Illustrator.

Jeremy worked under my supervision as a Graphic Illustrator from March 1998, until April 2001. His responsibilities included conducting research, developing concepts, preparing concept boards, and rendering final graphic illustrations for publication. In addition, he performed some administrative and clerical duties related to the maintenance of the company illustration database.

During the over three years that he reported to me, Jeremy proved himself to be a highly skilled and exceptionally talented graphic illustrator. He consistently produced superior quality work, on time, and within budget targets.

I was particularly impressed by Jeremy's ability to complete all of his work on time, even when he was multi-tasking on two or more major projects in parallel. Frequently, he even completed his assignments ahead of time. His research was invariably thorough and comprehensive, and his editorial concepts were consistently creative and always appropriate and timely.

Jeremy developed his own personal "signature" style of illustration that quickly became the preferred choice of a number of our most valued customers. Because of that, he was assigned as lead illustrator on a number of major projects where normally, he would have been a secondary resource. This gave him the opportunity to demonstrate his excellent team leadership and project management skills.

Overall, Jeremy is a conscientious, dedicated, and exemplary employee. I certainly think he has a bright future ahead of him in the editorial illustration field. Accordingly, I am pleased to recommend him for any intermediate to senior level position as an editorial graphic illustrator.

Sincerely,

Raymond S. Eaton
Director, Graphics Services

Recommendation Letter: Employment - Sample 5 (one project)

(print a Recommendation Letter on company letterhead paper)

July 27, 2002

Ms. Roberta Carnavon
Director, Administrative Services
Corporate Connection Inc.
128 Fifth Avenue
New York, NY, 10011

RE: Recommendation – Ingrid Heintzman

Dear Ms. Carnavon:

Ingrid Heintzman worked under my direct supervision for the six-month period, June through November 2001. Her role was that of Project Coordinator for the planning and implementation of a major international conference that was held in Toronto from October 8-10, 2001. On that project, I believe that I was able to develop a pretty fair idea of Ingrid's professional capabilities, as well as her primary personal attributes as they relate to the job.

Although relatively inexperienced in project management when she started, Ingrid was very quick to catch on to the required tools and techniques. Using state of the art project management software, she developed an extensive and detailed Project Work Plan which was the basic tool for project planning and status reporting/tracking. In addition, Ingrid developed a Project Accountability Matrix which became the primary day-to-day operational tool for assigning and monitoring staff resources assigned to the various project tasks.

As Project Coordinator Ingrid was responsible for organizing and chairing daily project review/status meetings. She performed this role with ease and was always well-prepared for the meetings. In addition, Ingrid functioned very well as a member of the project team and consistently dealt with difficult situations appropriately. She is well-organized and is always willing to put in extra time when required.

In addition to the above-mentioned project work, Ingrid was also asked to review and evaluate the Board's Contacts Database. On this project, she did an excellent job of supervising the two employees engaged in updating and modifying this important corporate database. I was particularly impressed with the thorough, well-written, and professional report that Ingrid prepared on her assessment of the database at the end of that project.

As a co-worker and colleague, Ingrid was outstanding. She was co-operative and positive at all times and was very well-liked by both her colleagues and the senior managers she dealt with. She has a very pleasant and positive demeanor and is a pleasure to work with.

In closing, based on my experience working with Ingrid Heintzman, I would recommend her very highly to you. I believe that her presence at the Junior/Intermediate Officer level would greatly benefit your organization. For further information, please contact me at (613) 772-4957.

Sincerely,

Robert Brady, M.B.A
Executive Director, Corporate Services

Recommendation Letter: Employment - Sample 6 (peer recommendation)

(print a Recommendation Letter from a private citizen on regular stationery)

Beverly C. Taylor
3200 75th Avenue
Landover, MD 20785
(301) 731-4754

December 10, 2002

Ms. Marilyn Joyner
Chief, Personnel Services
Liston Electronics Corp.
185 Parkway Dr.
Landover, MD, 20780

RE: Employment Recommendation – Ms. Francis Beresford

Dear Marilyn Joyner:

I was asked by Francis Beresford to write this letter to you based on my experience working closely with her for most of this year.

I had the fortunate opportunity to work closely with Francis Beresford for eight months earlier this year while she was employed at Brenkman Systems Inc.

Francis occupied the office adjacent to mine, and we collaborated on a number of projects. During the entire period, she was a pleasure to work with. I observed her to be a solid team player, a sincere and hardworking individual, as well as an excellent overall co-worker.

Francis worked very hard at all times, and frequently did more than her share of the work on our joint projects. She was an independent thinker and innovator, and often took the initiative to move things forward while we were waiting for senior management decisions.

I was happy to be able to work with Francis, since management invariably praised the projects that we completed as a team. In fact, on more than one occasion I made specific requests to work with Francis although I had been scheduled for other assignments.

Francis was well-liked by everyone in our office, both co-workers and management. She often went out of her way to be friendly and helpful to her colleagues.

Based on our eight months working together, I am pleased to recommend Francis for whatever position she may qualify for at your company. I believe she is the type of employee that any organization would be happy to have on their workforce.

Sincerely,

Beverly C. Taylor

Recommendation Letter: Employment - Sample 7 (short-term project)

(print a Recommendation Letter on company letterhead paper)

December 20, 2002

Mr. Adrian Singer
Project Manager
The Conference Organizers Inc.
5700 Orberlin Drive, Suite 200
San Diego, CA, 92121

Dear Mr. Singer:

Juanita Williams worked under my direct supervision for the seven-month period, May through November 2002. During that period she performed the dual role of Receptionist for the overall Agency, and Administrative Assistant for the Corporate Services Group. Supervising her in those capacities, I believe that I was able to develop a fair idea of Juanita's performance and capabilities, as well as the primary personal attributes which she brought to those jobs.

Although relatively inexperienced when she joined the Agency, Juanita quickly demonstrated that she was a fast-learner and a very willing worker. After a short adjustment period, she performed her primary role as Receptionist in a very efficient and professional manner. At this Agency, that job frequently requires interaction with course participants from many different countries who speak a number of languages, and have different cultural perspectives and attitudes. Juanita was astute at handling these people and situations with tact and diplomacy.

As mentioned, Juanita was also required to perform work as an Administrative Assistant in support of various Institute groups/projects. In this capacity, she always demonstrated that she was a quick learner and very adaptable to performing a wide variety of different tasks efficiently and effectively. She performed extremely well in what was often a multi-tasking situation, working for a number of different supervisors, while still handling her primary Receptionist duties. I was particularly impressed by how quickly and seamlessly she was able to provide support to the Financial/Accounting Group of the Agency, which involved learning the Institute's financial systems and processing varied and complex financial transactions.

On the personal attribute side, Juanita was truly a pleasure to work with. She displayed an extremely friendly, helpful, and outgoing demeanor at all times. As a result, she was very well-liked by both her colleagues and course participants. In fact, I would say that Juanita's pleasant and skilled manner in dealing with the Institute's multi-cultural clientele is likely to generate significant repeat business for the Agency. She has an intuitive understanding of the "client service" and "clients first" attitudes which are so necessary in business these days.

In closing, as I hope the above clearly attests, I would highly recommend Juanita Williams for positions similar to those she held with our organization. In addition, I believe that she demonstrated that she has the potential to perform even more complex and demanding duties.

For further information, please don't hesitate to contact me at (313) 913-1762.

Sincerely,

Mary Steinhart
Director, Administrative Services

Recommendation Letter: Employment - Sample 8 (part-time student)

(print a Recommendation Letter on corporate letterhead paper)

April 25, 2002

Ms. Diana Dumbrell
Recreation Director
Pinewood Lake Camp
Pinewood Lake, ON
H3P 4L2

<u>RE: Employment Recommendation - Chelsea Salzberg</u>

Dear Ms. Dumbrell:

Chelsea asked me to write this to you based on our working association over the past three summers. I understand she is applying for a Senior Program Co-ordinator position with you.

I have known Chelsea Salzberg since the summer of 1999. We first met when she became a volunteer counselor at the City's Pineview Day Camp for Kids. She volunteered that summer since she was not yet old enough to be a paid worker. She did this to both serve her community and to gain valuable counseling experience.

From the very beginning, Chelsea proved to be an eager and highly-motivated worker. During her first year with us she worked with the 5 to 8 year-olds and did a great job of keeping them busy with a variety of imaginative activities and crafts. Many of these group activities were Chelsea's own creation, and I had to spend very little time supervising her once I got her started. The kids loved her too. It was a great first summer.

During the summers of 2000 and 2001, Chelsea worked at the day camp as a paid counselor. The first year she was a regular Counselor and in 2000, she moved on to Senior Counselor duties.

I really can't say enough about how well Chelsea handled her duties those two summers. She was definitely my top performer. She has a special knack for communicating with kids in all age groups. They just seem to relate very well to her and hang on her every word. No doubt, this has a lot to do with Chelsea's unusually friendly and outgoing demeanor. Needless to say, she was very well liked by the kids, her peer counselors, and the City managers.

One particular strength that Chelsea demonstrated consistently, was her leadership ability. This became particularly apparent last year when she organized and supervised two off-site field trips. The trips were considered great successes by both participants and staff, and went smoothly.

Overall, Chelsea is a dedicated, hard-working counselor who always puts the needs of the kids before her own. She is a cooperative and willing employee, always ready to go the extra mile.

Accordingly, without hesitation I am pleased to recommend Chelsea Salzberg for the Senior Program Coordinator position at your camp. I have no doubts that she will do an excellent job.
Please call me at 732-1576 if you have any questions.

Sincerely,

Patricia Heywood
Recreation Program Director, City of Ottawa

Recommendation Letter: Employment - Sample 9 (community service)

(print a Recommendation Letter from a private citizen on regular stationery)

98 North Ridge Road
Minneapolis, MN, 55420

June 30, 2002

Dr. Alan Banting
Director, Adult Counselling Services
Holy Cross Memorial Hospital
453 South 6th Street – Admin. Bldg.
Minneapolis, MN, 55425

Dear Dr. Banting:

Thank you for your letter asking me for my assessment of Fred Smalling as possible member of your Adult Counseling Advisory Committee. It is my understanding that Fred provided my name to you as a possible reference.

I have known Fred for a little over 20 years, both as a neighbor and a fellow volunteer on many community projects. Shortly after we moved into the neighborhood in the early 1980s, I joined the Friendship Program at the hospital and discovered that the chairperson of that committee lived right across the street from me. It was Fred. Since then, we have had fairly regular contact.

Although we don't socialize that much as neighbors, I know Fred best through his work with the Police Association Assistance Program and through his involvement with the Friends of Schizophrenics group.

Based on my volunteer work with Fred over the past two decades, I am pleased to be able to recommend him as a member of your new committee. He is a dedicated, community-minded individual who puts helping others less fortunate than himself as his number one priority. One thing in particular that always amazed me about Fred is his ability to leave his stressful job with the police force at the end of the day and then freely give up two or three evenings of every week to the various causes he supports. Many weekends too. He's clearly an exemplary citizen.

Fred has an amazing ability to relate to people from all walks of life. He is also very smart and has excellent organizational and leadership abilities. Fred is almost always the one who takes charge and motivates both clients and volunteers. Having been so involved in community service work over the years, he is very knowledgeable about fund-raising techniques, and he has many contacts in his network. You might want to consider him seriously as overall Chair, or at least, Fund Raising Chair, on your committee.

In closing, I'm sure that Fred Smalling would be a valuable addition to you committee. I only hope that his involvement with that won't take him away from all of the good work that he already does for so many. You can reach me at 543-5678 if you have any questions.

Yours in service,

Bradley Finnegan

Recommendation Letter: Employment - Sample 10 (refusal to write one)

(print a Recommendation Letter on corporate letterhead paper)

September 10, 2002

Miranda Rasmussen
429-A Central Ave.
Cincinatti, OH, 45202

Dear Miranda:

Suzanne Trimble told me that you had called wondering if I would provide you with a letter of recommendation for a new position you are applying for.

I thank you for the honor, but after some consideration, I'm afraid I will have to decline to write you a letter. Believe me, it is nothing personal. As far as I know, your relatively brief stay with our company was a productive one for you and a pleasant one for your colleagues.

However, since you didn't report to me directly, I don't feel that I know you or your work well enough to be able to make a recommendation one way or another. I would suggest that you request a letter from Angela Goodall since she was your boss for your final six months with the company. Perhaps you have already done so.

Angela would be in a much better position to provide a fair assessment of your work performance during your stay with us. I'm sure she would be agreeable to writing you a letter.

Of course, if you are simply looking for someone to confirm your term of employment here, and your salary level, I suggest you ask Roger Simmons, the Director of Human Resources. I'm sure that his staff could get something like that out to you in a hurry.

I wish you the very best in the future.

Sincerely,

Kenneth Thomas
President and CEO

cc: Angela Goodall, Director of Marketing

COLLEGE-RELATED RECOMMENDATION LETTERS

Recommendation letters are usually required for entry into undergraduate and graduate programs at a college or university. Many graduate programs require two or more letters of recommendation as part of the mandatory program admission requirements.

In fact, even if a letter isn't specifically required for an undergraduate program application, it is still a good idea to attach at least one or two. These will make your application stand out from the others.

Normally, these program admission recommendation letters are written at the request of the program applicant by people who are familiar with that person's academic career to-date, and their future education and career aspirations.

For an undergraduate applicant, these letter-writers could include such people as: high school teacher, principal, or vice-principal, community leaders, volunteer program coordinators, clergy, part-time employers.

For graduate program applicants the typical recommendation letter-writer would be academics and professionals who have a solid direct knowledge of the work and character of the applicant: these people would typically be: undergraduate faculty members, administrators, academic supervisors, and professionals in the applicant's discipline.

Of course, it almost goes without saying that whoever writes these letters must be familiar enough with the applicant to be credible, and to be able to answer specific questions about their recommendation if contacted.

DRAFTING TIPS – COLLEGE-RELATED RECOMMENDATION LETTERS

Many of the tips for writing employment-related recommendation as well as reference letters also apply to these. So, please review those sections along with this one. However, pay close attention to the following tips because they include subtle differences that apply very specifically to college-related recommendation letters.

If you are asked by someone to write a college-related letter of recommendation for them, or if you need one written for you, here are some important points to keep in mind:

Make Sure You're The One

If you have been asked to write a recommendation letter for someone, it is important that you feel comfortable with the task. If you feel that you don't know the person and/or their academic achievements and aspirations well enough, you should decline, stating that as your reason. Also, you may find that it would be difficult for you to say very much positive about the person requesting the letter, in which case you should also decline.

Allow Plenty of Lead-Time

If you are the person requesting that someone draft a recommendation letter for you, give that person as much lead-time as you can. It's not fair to ask for a recommendation letter a day or two before it's required. I would say one week as an absolute minimum.

A person asked to write a recommendation letter at the very last minute has every right to refuse. Also, quality will suffer if the letter is rushed at the last minute.

Gather Background Information First

Before starting to write, you should have certain background information available. You'll need to know exactly to whom you are writing. You may also need the requestor to supply you with other relevant background information such as: resume/cv, recent transcripts, copies of academic papers, etc.

In the opening paragraph, list all of the background information such as: your organization name, position title, your relationship to the applicant, when and how you met, time-frame and dates covered, and any other relevant overall background information.

Write To A Specific Person

Recommendation letters for college and university programs should always be personalized. Even if the instructions you receive just provide a mailing address, make a point of finding out the name and title of a specific person to write to. Just check out the Web site of the institution and/or make a phone call.

Personalizing the letter will give you more credibility and will make yours stand out from the others. In other words, do not address one of these letters: "To whom it may concern" or "Dear Admissions Secretary."

Get Input From The Requestor

In addition to the basic background information already mentioned, you may need some additional personal information from the requestor/applicant. You might want to ask them to provide you with a checklist summary of key points that they would like you to cover. In addition, you might want to get clarification from them as to their academic and career aspirations.

Cover The Entire Person

The recommendation letter should address all aspects of the applicant that relate to their ability to perform in the program being applied for. Many colleges and universities provide actual checklists of the categories to be covered in recommendation letters. In fact, research into this has revealed that there are literally hundreds of different checklists like this, depending on the institution involved.

Following is a "typical" list of typical attributes and characteristics that would normally be covered in a recommendation letter for a graduate or undergraduate program:

- Intellectual ability
- Knowledge of the field
- Employment and/or academic potential
- Motivation
- Initiative and creativity
- Work habits
- Seriousness of approach
- Emotional makeup and maturity
- Communication skills and abilities
- Adaptability

I have even seen attribute checklists that go as far as requiring information on "personal grooming and hygiene" and "appropriate eye contact"!

Use your own judgment as to what makes sense in a particular context, as to how far you should go.

Be Specific and Give Examples

It will be helpful if your letter rates your applicant relative to their peers. For this you can use relativity phrases such as: average, very good, excellent, or below average. If you can quantify it would also be helpful. For example, "Robert's overall grade point average puts him in the top 5% of the class".

Always try to give specific examples rather than just making open-ended generalizations. For example, "Daphne's ability as a researcher is outstanding as can be seen in her recent paper titled 'From Quantum Physics To Eternity' a copy of which is attached". Or, "Rob's strong communication skills were highlighted when he presented his paper on 'The Psychology of Addiction" at last year's Regional Conference."

Avoid Controversial Statements/Terminology

Do not make statements that you cannot clearly support with facts. For example, statements such as "I believe Frank displays this tendency because he is the product of a dysfunctional background" are clearly not acceptable.

Make sure you avoid using any words or terminology that could be construed as discriminatory such as: race, color, religion, political affiliation, sex, sexual orientation, age, physical appearance, handicaps, marital, or parental status.

Use Active, Powerful Words

Neutral words such as good, nice, satisfactory, fair, reasonable, etc. should be avoided. Use active, descriptive words and terms such as: intelligent, assertive, initiator, self-starter, motivated, hard-working, cooperative, productive, creative, articulate, leader, communicator, team player, innovative, effective, efficient, honest, dependable, mature, etc.

Review The Final Product

Before signing your letter, do a final careful review. Check all spelling and grammar and make sure the terminology used is appropriate. Read it out loud to yourself and imagine being the recipient. Is it fair and balanced? Does it truly convey what you believe and want to say about the person who you are recommending? If not, revise it.

SAMPLE TEMPLATES - COLLEGE-RELATED RECOMMENDATION LETTERS

The following pages contain five (5) fully-formatted real-life sample templates of recommendation letters written for actual college-related situations.

Recommendation Letter: College-Related - Sample 1 (undergraduate applicant)

(print a Recommendation Letter on company letterhead paper)

October 25, 2002

Ms. Jillian Shepperd
Director of Admissions
Admissions and Recruitment Office
MacDonald University
1449 Dorchester Ave. W., Rm 451
Montreal, QC, H3A 1T4

Dear Ms. Shepperd:

I am very pleased to write this recommendation on behalf of Layla Bell.

Layla has been a student in the accelerated liberal arts program at Holymount High for her entire five years of high school. During that period I have observed her grow into a poised and accomplished young woman. She is an exceptional student with excellent grades resulting from diligent work habits.

Layla has superior interpersonal skills and works equally well independently or in a group setting. She also displays good leadership skills when involved in group projects. She is very well liked and respected by both her peers and her teachers.

Among her many service activities at the school, Layla was a coach of the junior track team for the past two years and she was a member of the senior cross-country team. She also took part in the Mentoring Program and helped a number of juniors navigate their way through their first year of high school. In addition, Layla was involved in organizing a number of fund-raising projects at the school, including a team marathon event that raised over $5,000 for cancer research.

Layla has shown an ongoing interest in world affairs and international development. It is my understanding that she intends to pursue an Honors degree in Political Science or Sociology. She has traveled extensively and has written outstanding reports with observations on conditions she has witnessed throughout the world.

I believe that Layla Bell has tremendous potential as a student and I feel quite confident that she would be an asset to both student life and academics at MacDonald University.

Yours truly,

Allan S. Fenton
Vice-Principal

Recommendation Letter: College-Related - Sample 2 (mature student applicant)

(print a Recommendation Letter on company letterhead paper)

December 15, 2002

Professor Reiner Holzman
Director, Teaching Studies
Boston University Center
115 Beacon St., Rm. 489
Boston, MA, 02110

<u>**Re: Recommendation Letter - Deanna Daryna**</u>

Dear Professor Holzman:

I have been asked to write this letter for Deanna Daryna as one of the requirements for her admission to the Teaching English As A Second Language (TESL) program.

I have known Deanna for a total of fifteen (15) years. In 1986 we started out together as colleagues in the advertising department of Reader's World Magazine. We worked together there for a period of six years during which I got to know her quite well. Then, in 1995 Deanna moved to our Atlanta office for two years to take part in a special assignment team as the company started to gear-up its Internet presence. When Deanna returned to head office in 1998 she became my employee since I had been promoted to Director of Advertising Operations the previous year.

Accordingly, I know Deanna in a professional capacity primarily as an advertising copywriter and direct marketing expert. What I can tell you about her is that, in those two areas, she is among the very best in the business. She has a gift for copywriting, and her creative mind was responsible for some of the most successful marketing campaigns that Reader's World has ever implemented.

Deanna was hand-picked by senior management to work in Atlanta with the Internet Presence Project Team. As team leader, she headed up a small group responsible for adapting our direct mail campaigns to the Internet environment. The company implemented that team's strategy in early 2000 and now Reader's World is among the top three publishing companies on the Web.

During the dot com meltdown in 2000, our company went through a major downsizing exercise. Deanna decided that she wanted to take an early retirement package and do something different with her life. I was not at all surprised when she told me that she wanted to go back to school and learn to teach English as a second language. In our early years at Reader's World I had often seen Deanna in the teaching role as she trained new employees from all over the world about how to implement the company's mailing campaigns. I could see that she very much enjoyed that teaching role and how well-suited she was to it. She had a special knack for communicating with employees from our regional offices in developing countries. So, in a sense, Deanna's new path in TESL is a natural progression from her training work with the company.

In my opinion Deanna Daryna is an exceptionally bright and hardworking individual who throws herself enthusiastically into what ever she undertakes. Accordingly, I have no hesitation whatsoever in recommending Deanna as a participant in your TESL program.

Sincerely,

Robert Jamieson
Director, Advertising Operations

Recommendation Letter: College-Related - Sample 3 (undergraduate, first job)

(print a Recommendation Letter on corporate letterhead paper)

December 1, 2002

Mr. Roland Zimmerman
General Manager and Editor
Windy City Publishing
Clarkson Press Building, 12th Flr.
200 East Huron Street
Chicago, IL, 60610

Dear Mr. Zimmerman:

I am pleased to be able to write this letter of recommendation for Valerie Douglas. I understand that she has applied for a job with you as a manuscript reviewer.

I have known Valerie since she entered Lakeland College as a freshman three years ago. Over the years I have gotten to know her as a student in two of my classes and also as her department head.

From the very first year, Valerie impressed me in a number of ways. She is a verious serious student but can also be very enthusiastic about everything she does. I first met Valerie when she was a student in my introductory english literature class. She immediately struck me as a very earnest person who became increasingly excited about the course material as the semester progressed.

I was very pleased when Valerie asked me to sign her "intent to become an English major" form. Since then, I have watched her use both her seriousness and enthusiasm to develop into an outstanding english major. She possesses an excellent knowledge base in english literature and has developed strong analytical, critiquing, and writing skills.

Most recently, Valerie participated in my Early Classics Seminar series, and her performance in the class was excellent. Her contributions included: she wrote three strong papers on topics related to the lives of classics authors, she collaborated with three of her classmates on a skillfully written "period novella", she participated actively in three group discussions, and she led a well-prepared and professionally delivered group presentation in class.

I believe it is Valerie's strong work ethic, coupled with her meticulous attention to detail that allows her to produce such high quality papers. Her ability to work well with others, even under stress, allows her to get the most out of group assignments. Her strong performance as leader of the group presentation was a result of rigorous preparation and her excellent oral communication skills which allowed her to highlight how well she knew her subject.

If you are seeking someone who has consistently demonstrated the following skills, abilities and characteristics during her undergraduate career, then I suggest you give Valerie your full consideration.

- Carries out projects successfully
- Deals effectively with a wide variety of people
- Gathers and organizes information from multiple sources
- Works effectively as a team member
- Handles conflict successfully

- Shows initiative, creativity, and persistence
- Demonstrates effective time management
- Speaks articulately and persuasively
- Writes clearly and precisely

In summary, I am pleased to recommend Valerie Douglas to you without reservation. If you have any questions regarding the above, please don't hesitate to call me at (312) 335-9747.

Sincerely,

Donald R. Atkinson, Ph.D.
Professor and Department Head

Recommendation Letter: College-Related - Sample 4 (graduate applicant)

(print Recommendation Letter on corporate letterhead paper)

November 20, 2002

Ms. Catherine Halstat
Assistant Head
Psychology Department
Health Research Center
Midwestern College
1345 College Park Road
Minneapolis, MN, 55450

Dear Ms. Halstat:

This letter is in support of Jason Fairbank's application for admission to your graduate program. Jason is currently a senior psychology major at Midwestern. I have known him since we met in his senior year of high school during a Midwestern familiarization session. We made contact again as soon as he enrolled as a freshman and I have followed his progress ever since.

I have been at Midwestern since 1984 and rarely have I seen a psychology major with as much going for him as Jason has. I believe he has a high potential for success in graduate school.

Jason's greatest strength is his ability to perform research. As a sophomore, he enrolled in Internet-Enabled Research Methods, our senior-level research course. Students in this course must complete a full research project (from literature review to final paper) in only one semester, and they must present the results of their research at the meeting of the Midwest Psychology Research Symposium that is held annually at the University of Southern Illinois.

In my opinion, Jason's presentation was among the top three given at the conference that year. His clarity and composure during the presentation, and his poise and ability to think on his feet during the question period that followed were truly remarkable for a sophomore. He presented another paper at that conference in his junior year which was even better than his sophomore paper. Jason conducts himself very professionally at these conferences and is particularly adept at networking with students and faculty from other institutions to gain more insight into their research and share his own findings.

One of Jason's papers at last year's conference was a presentation of a new student evaluation form that he and several other students developed as a research team. That presentation went over so well that Jason and his team members were asked by the chairperson of the conference to present their research at last spring's National College Conference. They were the first students in Midwestern's history to present at the National Conference. After that, their evaluation methodology was approved by the board and the faculty and has been in use college-wide ever since. This is a good demonstration of Jason's ability to lead a cooperative team effort, a quality that I'm sure will serve him well in your graduate program.

Jason has taken four courses classes from me over the years: Introduction to Psychology, Social Psychology, Developmental Psychology, and The Psychology of Addictions. He has performed exceptionally well in all of them. He is an intelligent, enthusiastic, well-prepared, well-spoken, and assertive individual who gets a lot out of his classes and also gives back a considerable amount through his active participation. His comments in class are always timely, relevant, and valuable in summarizing the discussion or stimulating it to go in new directions. His writing is clear, concise, and articulate.

Jason also has excellent computer skills and his minor is in information technology. He is a self-starter who can work independently with little or no supervision. One particular strength that Jason has is the ability to integrate and synthesize information from a variety of sources to produce novel, yet realistic, creative interpretations and conclusions. He used this gift especially well in my Developmental Psychology course in which he scored exceptionally well in his independent project work.

One of Jason's most remarkable traits is his deep-rooted sense of moral and ethical responsibility. We have had many conversations about the ethical climate of both Midwestern College and US universities and colleges in general. As a result, Jason undertook a major research project that deals with the issue of academic integrity. One of the papers that he presented at last year's National Conference entitled "Dishonesty in Academia – Myth or Reality?" looked at the various types of typical academic dishonest behavior (e.g., cheating and plagiarism) and estimated their degree of prevalence at both Midwestern and at other campuses across the country. Jason was recently invited by the President of this college to present his findings on this at an upcoming Regional College Forum.

As you know, success in graduate school is a function of many variables including intelligence, motivation, communication skills, and personal traits. Although often overlooked in letters of recommendation, this last factor may well be one of the most important at the graduate studies level.

As an individual, Jason is an extremely well-rounded person. He is likeable, straightforward, down-to-earth, confident, and generally, a pleasant person to be around. He is very well-liked and held in high regard by both his peers and members of the faculty. When he has the time, Jason serves as a volunteer mentor in the Freshman Assistance Program and off-campus he is involved in a number community fund-raising projects. Somehow, in the midst of all of these academic and community service activities, he still manages to find the time to play squash. In fact, he was a member of Midwestern's Intercollegiate Squash Team that placed third at the Regional Championships earlier this year.

In conclusion, based on the foregoing it should be clear that I regard Jason Fairbanks as an outstanding individual in every sense of the word. Accordingly, I recommend Jason to you for acceptance into your graduate studies program, without hesitation. I believe he is exactly the type of undergraduate student that I would accept into a graduate program if I were making such a decision. In my opinion, Jason has unlimited potential and will eventually go far as a professional psychologist in the coming years.

Sincerely,

Frederick Wyatt, Ph.D.
Department Head

Recommendation Letter: College-Related - Sample 5 (scholarship applicant)

(print a Recommendation Letter on corporate letterhead paper)

August 31, 2002

Margaret A. Smeltzer
Chairperson
Scholarship Selection Committee
Pacific Coast University
2705 Valleyview Drive, Rm. 205
San Diego, CA, 92120

Dear Mrs. Smeltzer:

I am writing this letter in support of Daniel Kim's nomination for the 2002-03 California Human Resources Society Scholarship.

I have known Daniel since he entered PCU as a freshman three years ago. Since that time I have come to know him very well as his teacher in four of his courses, and through various academic and extracurricular interactions. I am writing this because it is my sincere belief that he is eminently qualified as a deserving recipient of your scholarship. Over the past three years he has demonstrated to me that he possesses exceptionally high levels of academic ability, motivation, and potential for contributions to the field of human resources management.

Daniel earned a grade of "A" in all four courses that he took from me: Psychology - An Introduction, The Science of Psychology, Developmental Psychology, and Research Studies in Psychology. Please note that the criterion for an "A" in all four of these classes is only attained by receiving 95% of all possible points. The Science of Psychology is an extremely rigorous course, and fewer than 2% of students have ever received an "A" in this subject in the 15 years that I have been teaching it. His performance in Developmental Psychology was just as remarkable. He received perfect scores on 10 of 12 tests and earned 98 out of a possible of 100 on his term paper.

Daniel's current accumulated GPA is 3.87 (out of 4.0) and his GPA in psychology classes is 4.0. He has never received a grade lower than an "A" since his freshman year. He will graduate "with Honors" next year. This superior level of academic performance indicates an exceptional understanding of his subject material. With knowledge, skills, and abilities at this level, Daniel should go far in his field in the future. I believe he plans to attend graduate school, and we are currently looking at his options in this area.

One of Daniel's key strengths is his ability to analyze, integrate, and synthesize information from a wide variety of disparate sources and to apply the essence of this information to an important topic. His term paper, titled "The History of Cognitive Dissonance and Its Prevalence In The Corporate Workplace" is an excellent example of this ability. A copy of that paper is attached.

Students writing papers were asked to accomplish the following three objectives:

- Document the history of a particular area of psychology in which you have a particular interest.

- Explain a controversial issue that continues to exist within this area.

- Take and defend a specific position on this controversial issue.

As you will see if you have the time to even skim the attached, Daniel's paper is meticulously well-researched, argued, and written. It was by far the best in the class. His work was also very well organized and his writing style was simple, clear, and precise. His discussions were thoughtful and the rationale for his arguments were well laid-out. His research was exceedingly thorough, and he cited some 38 sources although only 15 were required.

Daniel's paper is the ideal precursor for a major research project in human resource management that he plans to undertake next year on Morals and Ethics In the Workplace. That course requires the completion of an original empirical research project with the aid of computer applications software at each stage (i.e., bibliographic search, statistical analysis, graphics production, and word processing). The final requirement of this course is the presentation of the completed paper at the annual Regional Undergraduate Research Conference. I have absolutely no doubt that Daniel will produce a research paper that reflects positively on himself, our department, and PCU.

Daniel is the perfect example of an exceptional student whose actions speak louder that his words. Because of his academic prowess and his achievements to-date, in the PCU Psychology Department, Daniel "walks softly but carries a big stick", as the expression goes. He is highly esteemed by his peers and the faculty members. Both groups are aware that he is a young man of considerable talent, intelligence, and motivation who knows how to go the extra mile and contribute his skills to the group in a quiet, professional manner.

As an active and committed member of the PCU Psychology Club, Daniel has set a new standard for club activities. His leadership abilities have not gone unnoticed. This past year he was elected National Secretary of the American Association of Undergraduate Psychology Clubs (AAUPC). He has also been re-elected President of his local chapter for next year.

As teachers, every once in a few years we may be fortunate enough to teach someone who we believe has what it takes to go on and make a major difference in their field. I believe that Daniel is one of those rare individuals.

In closing, without hesitation I would like to recommend that Daniel Kim be chosen as the recipient of the California Human Resources Society Scholarship, for 2002-03. This young man deserves it.

Sincerely,

Mathew Houston, Ph.D.
Professor and Department Head

attachment

REFERENCE LETTERS

These are more general letters that are often requested by employees when they leave the employ of an organization. Normally factual in nature, they are usually addressed, "to whom it may concern" and provide basic information such as: work history, dates of employment, positions held, academic credentials, etc.

Reference letters sometimes contain a general statement (as long as a positive one can be made) about the employee's work record with the company that they are leaving. Employees often submit these letters with job applications in the hope that the letter will reflect favorably on their chances for the new position.

Character reference letters are sometimes required by employers when hiring individuals to perform personal or residential services such as child care, domestic services, etc. These letters are usually drafted by a former employer and deal with such characteristics as honesty, dependability, and work ethic/performance.

DRAFTING TIPS – REFERENCE LETTERS

The information in this section is very similar to the tips listed earlier under employment-related recommendation letters, but there are some subtle differences specific to reference letters.

I chose to repeat some of the information here so that this would be a stand-alone section and you won't have to flip back-and-forth and get confused between reference letters and recommendation letters. (It's confusing enough as it is!).

Remember; although a reference letter is one "type" of letter of recommendation, it is somewhat different from the recommendation letters we covered earlier.

Reference letters are much more general in nature and are usually addressed "to whom it may concern". Whereas recommendation letters are more personalized and detailed and should, almost without exception, be addressed to a specific person.

If you are asked by someone to write a "letter of reference" for them, here are a few important points to keep in mind:

Make Sure You're The Right One

If you feel that you don't know the person well enough or are not the appropriate person you should decline. This is not as critical a situation as it is for recommendation letters since your reference letter will be more general in nature and not directed to a specific person.

However, remember that your personal "John Henry" will be in the signature block.

Typically, if an employment-related reference letter, you would be asked to write it by someone who is leaving your organization to take another job. Normally, you would have a certain moral obligation to supply such a letter.

But watch out! I recently read an article stating that lawyers for some big firms are advising their corporate clients not to commit themselves to paper in general reference letters for fear of later legal repercussions in cases where they might give a good reference and then later the employee somehow screws up.

To me, this is paranoid thinking. But we all know what lawyers are like when it comes to covering rear ends. My advice is; just make sure that whatever you write is honest and fair.

Start With The Background Parameters

As mentioned above, for a reference letter you will normally not be writing to any particular person. It's usually addressed "To whom it may concern". In the opening paragraph provide all of the background information such as: your relationship to the person, organization name, position titles, time-frame and dates covered by your assessment, and any other relevant background information.

In fact, for most reference letters you shouldn't have to get much more specific than that.

Get Additional Input From Requestor

If you feel you need more information, don't hesitate to ask the requestor for a copy of their resume/cv. In addition, if you have access to them, you may want to have a quick review of recent performance evaluations.

You can also ask the requestor to jot down some key points they would like you to mention if possible (at your discretion). This would include things like highlighting their work and accomplishments on a special project and/or their participation on a special task force.

Don't Get Too Specific

Since a reference letter is somewhat general and open-ended in nature, don't go overboard with specific traits and details about the person you are writing about. It will be helpful to use meaningful job-performance-related terms and words, although in a much more general sense than one would in a recommendation letter.

If it's employment-related, your reference letter should address all or most of the areas of the person that are job-performance-related, but in a general sense. Specific examples and details are less necessary than in a regular recommendation letter.

For example, such statements as "I observed Wendy to be a hard-working, highly-effective team participant, with strong communication skills" would suffice.

Avoid Controversial Terminology

As with recommendation letters, make sure you avoid using any words or terminology that could be construed as discriminatory such as: race, color, religion, political affiliation, sex, sexual orientation, age, physical appearance, handicaps, marital or parental status, etc.

Use Active, Powerful Words

Neutral words such as good, nice, satisfactory, fair, reasonable, etc. should be avoided.

Use active, descriptive words and terms such as: intelligent, assertive, initiator, self-starter, motivated, cooperative, productive, hard-working, creative, articulate, leader, communicator, team player, innovative, effective, efficient, honest, dependable, mature, etc.

Review The Final Product

Before signing your letter, do a final careful review. Check all spelling and grammar and make sure the terminology used is appropriate. Read it out loud to yourself and imagine being the recipient. Is it fair and balanced? Does it truly convey what you believe and want to say about the person who you are recommending? If not, revise it.

SAMPLE TEMPLATES - REFERENCE LETTERS

The following pages contain five (5) real-life templates of reference letters written for various situations.

Reference Letter: Sample 1 (employment)

(print an Employment Reference Letter on company letterhead stationery)

July 15, 2002

RE: Employment Reference – Tony Rocco

To whom it may concern:

This is to confirm that Tony Rocco worked under my direct supervision as an Insurance Sales Representative from January 1999 to October 2001.

During this period Tony progressed from sales initiation trainee to fully certified sales representative by the time he left for another job.

I would say that Tony is a hard working individual who learns quickly. He is generally cooperative and can perform well as a member of a team, although he prefers to work independently. He communicates very well orally and is working hard to improve his writing skills. I saw considerable improvement in this area during the last year he was with us.

As a sales professional, Tony was always above the 50th percentile of performers on my sales team. Since he started from scratch only two years ago, and most of his colleagues were highly experienced with strong, established networks, I would say that Tony achieved a lot in his early years as a sales representative.

So, based on what I observed during my two years with Tony, I believe he has excellent potential to become a high-performing sales professional in the insurance business.

For further information, I can be reached at (514) 989-0779.

Sincerely,

Jannik Soberman
Director, Insurance Sales Operations

Reference Letter: Sample 2 (character, friend)

(Character Reference Letter can be printed on company letterhead or standard paper)

501 Kemper Ave.
St. Louis, MO, 63139

October 14, 2002

RE: Character Reference – Jason Sunderland

To whom it may concern:

The purpose of this is to provide a character reference for Mr. Jason Sunderland who I have known as a classmate, roommate, and friend for a period of five years.

I first met Jason in our freshman year at Adirondack College. We were both studying a general arts program there and became acquainted through a number of common classes that we shared. By second year, we had become friends and decided to take an off-campus apartment together. We shared that living arrangement until we both graduated last year.

Accordingly, having gotten to know Jason so well over the past few years, I believe puts me in a position to provide you with a pretty accurate assessment of his character.

As a student, Jason was a hard-working and highly committed to his education. I believe that his excellent transcripts will attest to that fact. In addition, he was quite involved in a number of extra-curricular activities including the track and field team and the school newspaper. In fact, in his last two years he was Assistant Editor of the "Campus Inquirer." Outgoing, and always willing to help someone out, Jason was very popular with his fellow students.

As a roommate, Jason was a great choice. He was very neat and tidy at all times and he liked things in the apartment to be kept orderly. He made a point of cleaning his own room and the common living areas on a regular basis. He socialized occasionally at home but was always respectful of my needs, and he and his guests kept the noise down and ended their activities at a reasonable hour.

As a friend, Jason Sunderland is a standout. He is a loyal, honest, considerate, and supportive individual who has the ability to see and understand things from another person's perspective. He is a great direct communicator and knows how to raise and discuss common living issues and problems in a non-threatening manner. He is hyper-sensitive and is always tuned into how another person might "feel" in a given situation. He likes to have fun too. During our years at school we maintained an ongoing friendly rivalry on the squash courts.

To tell the truth, I really can't think of anything of consequence on the negative side of the personality ledger when it comes to Jason. All in all, I would have to say that Jason Sunderland is a fine, well-balanced person with an abundance of positive qualities.

Sincerely,

Ronald Marrion

Reference Letter: Sample 3 (character, general)

(Recommendation Letter from a private citizen is printed on regular stationery)

9528 Carling Ave.
Apt. 1508
Ottawa, Ontario
K2B 8M5

January 25, 2002

RE: Character Reference - Manuela Gonzalez

To whom it may concern:

I have known Manuela Gonzalez since January 2000 when she began living-in with my ex-wife and caring for my daughter Charlotte.

Due to a divorce, I don't live in the same house as Manuela and my daughter, but I believe that over the past 20 months or so, I have had enough contact with her, both directly and indirectly (through my daughter's behavior), to be able to possess a reasonably accurate impression of her attributes and character.

Accordingly, based on all my personal dealings with Manuela (as well as comments made by Charlotte's mother), I find her to be a very kind, loving, and caring individual. I am very comforted to have such a person responsible for the day-to-day care of my daughter. In addition, I have also noted that Manuela is hard-working, responsible, conscientious, and honest. She has displayed good judgment, tactfulness, diplomacy, and co-operation in all of the contacts I have had with her.

Therefore, based on my knowledge of her, I would not hesitate to state that Manuela Gonzalez is a very dependable individual of seemingly impeccable character.

If you require further information, please don't hesitate to contact the undersigned at (819) 997-4295 or (613) 232-4158.

Sincerely,

Peter R. Shannon

Reference Letter: Sample 4 (former customer)

(Corporate Reference Letter is printed on corporate letterhead stationery)

3005 19th Street, NE
Calgary, AB
T2E 6Y9

November 20, 2002

RE: Customer Reference – Thompson Graphics Inc.

To whom it may concern:

I have been asked to write this letter of reference because our company will no longer be operating its printing plant that has served Thompson Graphics Inc. for more than a decade.

Thompson Graphics has been one of our top customers for the past 15 years. Accordingly, I have no hesitation in recommending them as a company to do business with.

In addition to doing business with his company for many years, Ray Thompson and I go back to our university days over 25 years ago. So, I can also vouch for him as a great individual and a concerned and active citizen in this community.

As far as a company to do business with, Thompson Graphics is one of the best that we have ever dealt with. Its practice was always to pay our printing invoices within the 30-day time limit. We did significant amounts of business, especially during the past 5 years, and I cannot recall a late-payment situation involving that company. Billing disputes were rare, and those only required some minor additional documentation for clarification and resolution.

Thompson was one of the best companies that I have ever dealt with from a change-order and work scheduling perspective. We maintained a close communication with the company's production people and they always kept us apprised of their upcoming workload, so that scheduling jobs on our presses was never a problem. In addition, Thompson's graphics people always provided us with high quality finished artwork, and it was unusual for additional changes to be made after the plates had been produced.

Based on our experience, any printing company should be very pleased to be the one that Thompson Graphics chooses to do business with once we have closed our doors.

Sincerely,

Stewart Johannsen
President and CEO

Reference Letter: Sample 5 (explain departure)

(Corporate Reference Letter is printed on corporate letterhead stationery)

395 North Summit Street
Arkansas City, KS
67005

December 15, 2002

RE: Reason For Leaving – Susan Williams

To whom it may concern:

The purpose of this is to explain why Susan Williams left our company after less than one year of employment.

Unfortunately, Susan is an innocent victim of corporate restructuring and downsizing. When we hired Susan as an online advertising specialist 11 months ago we had high hopes that the Internet-based economy would quickly pick up, and that Susan would be a part of our move to the next level in the industry.

Things did not turn around as quickly as we had hoped. So, in August our Board of Directors decided to impose a major restructuring and downsizing program on the online operations of the company, particularly in marketing and advertising. Susan was one of the people in the advertising department with the least amount of seniority, so we had to let her go.

This is to confirm that during the period Susan Williams worked with us we found her performance to be above average. In fact, the head of our advertising department tells me that he would re-hire Susan in a hurry if our fortunes turned around again.

If you require further information, I can be reached at (316) 442-0955.

Sincerely,

Margaret Amaroso
Director, Human Resources

COMMENDATION LETTERS

Commendation letters are unsolicited letters, which typically commend an employee to their supervisor or organization for something outstanding or noteworthy that the employee has done. Normally, the employee would have to do something "above and beyond" what is routinely expected of them in their job to warrant such a letter.

Typically, these letters are written by co-workers, or managers from another area of the organization who were suitably impressed while supervising the person on a short-term project.

Commendation letters are also often written in the community service sector when citizens or organizations believe that an individual has made an exceptional contribution in serving the public as a volunteer.

DRAFTING TIPS – COMMENDATION LETTERS

For general letter writing tips, please refer back to the section earlier in this guide titled "Letter Writing Guidelines".

The main thing that differentiates commendation letters from other types of recommendation letters is that they are almost always spontaneous and unsolicited, and normally come as a pleasant surprise to both the subject of the letter and its recipient.

Although there can be exceptions to this. For example, when someone is asked to write a letter of commendation so that the subject can be nominated for a formal award.

Following are a few tips to keep in mind when drafting a commendation letter for someone:

Think About It Carefully

Before writing an unsolicited commendation letter make sure in your own mind that it is truly warranted. This is not to discourage writing one of course, but they are meant to recognize a truly exceptional act or situation, well above the normal call of duty. Just think about it carefully and make sure it is the right thing to do under the circumstances. Once one is written and sent, you can't take it back.

Make sure that you are in a safe position to write such a letter. For example, if you are relatively new to the organization, you might want to wait a bit and do some research before you write such a letter. There could be lots of historical factors at play, some of which you may be unaware.

Do Some Basic Checking

In an organizational setting, before sending a commendation letter about someone it would be a good idea to get a hold of that person's job description to make sure that what you think is exceptional is a not simply a mandatory duty in their job description.

In fact, I would suggest once you have done your basic checking and are convinced that you want to go ahead, before you do, you might want to run the idea past the person's supervisor just to make sure you aren't stepping on someone's toes or are acting on incomplete information. If it is truly a situation that warrants a commendation letter, the subject's boss will normally be pleased about the positive cudos that will be going to the employee. (After all, it's also an indirect compliment to the subject's boss).

Get Proper Background Information

If the commendation letter you are writing involves an employee in an organization, you need to make sure you get the details right. After all, your letter will be passed around senior management in the organization and it will be placed on the employee's personnel file, permanently. In addition, the employee will more than likely use it as reference material when applying for promotions or other jobs in the future.

So, make sure you address it to the appropriate person and title. That is usually the employee's direct supervisor. Check that the details such as position titles and the spelling of names are correct.

Brace Yourself For Repercussions

This may be a bit sad, but in a typical medium to large organization, it is often a reality. No matter how well-intentioned you may be in writing your commendation letter, there will be those who are angry, upset, or resentful.

Yes, that's right. In my 25+ years working in a variety of organizations, both large and small, I learned that they are great incubators for the polishing and festering of the human ego.

The vast majority of people who become aware of your commendation letter will be happy for the recipient and wish them well. Nevertheless, there will also be those who resent it. Some people may regard you as suspect for writing such a letter, wondering what your hidden agenda is. Others will be acting out their jealousy wondering why they've never received such a commendation themselves.

Even if you're a manager, you could still be resented by other managers. They might not like the fact that you've taken the time to write such a letter for your employee, and feel that it makes them look bad in front of their own employees.

But don't let any of this stop you. If you think it is the right thing to do, go ahead and write that commendation letter.

SAMPLE TEMPLATES - COMMENDATION LETTERS

The following pages contain a number of commendation letter templates written for various real-life situations.

Commendation Letter: Sample 1 (corporate)

(Corporate Commendation normally printed on corporate memo letterhead stationery)

MEMORANDUM

Date: November 31, 2002

From: Monica Bates

To: Pablo Cassavetes
Director, Research Support Programs

Subject: Commendation – Hubert McConnell – Freight Transport Demand Project

The purpose of this is to officially commend Hubert McConnell for his exceptional contribution throughout his assignment to the Freight Transport Demand Project (FTDP).

As you know, Hubert has been working on special assignment with the FTDP team for the past eight months. Now that he is about to return to your part of the organization I wanted to make sure that he gets some recognition for his significant and exceptional contributions to the project.

As a junior econometrician, Hubert's role in the project was pivotal to its timely and successful completion. It was Hubert who worked long hours, numerous nights and weekends with his small team of researchers, first specifying, and then testing the thousands of equations that had to be run. The quality of Hubert's written work was also exceptional. His regression analysis summaries were always very well written and rarely required revision.

As a colleague and project team member, Hubert was also outstanding. His upbeat enthusiasm for the project was infectious, and he seemed to motivate the entire project team. He was very well –liked by all team members, and in effect he became "unofficial" deputy project manager.

In closing, I would like to say that I have worked with many junior economists and econometricians over the years and have never run across one who was as professional and productive as Hubert McConnell was on the FTDP. I believe that the organization as a whole should recognize his exceptional contribution to a major project.

Please let me know if you have any questions or comments.

Catherine Potvin
Director, Econometric Research

cc: Hubert McConnell
Personnel file – H. McConnell

Commendation Letter: Sample 2 (customer service)

(Commendation from a private citizen normally printed on standard stationery)

4590 Green Avenue
Montreal, QC

September 20, 2002

Ms. Vivien Wong
Manager, Guest Services
Mount Royal Hotel
4900 Sherbrooke Street
Montreal, H5S 3T7

<u>RE: Exceptional Service – Mr. Eduardo Perez</u>

Dear Ms. Wong:

My name is Paul Kubecki. I have been a member of your hotel's health and fitness club for over five years. I am writing this to you in your capacity as manager responsible for the club.

The sole purpose of this letter is to draw your attention to the exceptional level of service that has been provided by Mr. Eduardo Perez since he joined the staff of the health club, some 18 months ago. I normally wouldn't take the time to write a letter like this, but in Eduardo's case, I just had to because he has made such a difference to the level of service that members now receive.

From the day he joined the team at the club it was clear that Eduardo was different from those who had preceded him. It was obvious from the beginning that he has a clear understanding of what customer service is all about, and he knows how to deliver it to club members.

Among many other things, Eduardo is extremely courteous, thoughtful, and kind in all of his dealings with members. In addition, he is very effective in running club matters. For example, previously, when a machine would break down (i.e. a treadmill) it would take anywhere from 1 to 2 weeks for it to be repaired due to lack of follow-up by health club staff. Now, when a machine breaks down, Eduardo makes it his personal mission to see that things are followed-up. Since he arrived, repairs are always done within 24 to 48 hours.

Before Eduardo, it was a common occurrence for the water coolers to be left unfilled and the tissue boxes that should be kept outside of the squash courts would never be replaced without members complaining. Now with Eduardo in charge, these small but annoying things just don't happen anymore. He has instituted a "walk around" system whereby members of the health club staff must check all facilities at the beginning of their shift to see if anything needs attention.
This has made a big difference and has definitely been noticed by members.

I have discussed my intention to write this letter with a number of regular members and they enthusiastically supported the idea that Eduardo be acknowledged for his exceptional efforts. We trust that Eduardo Perez will somehow be recognized for delivering a superior level of customer service to members of the Mount Royal Hotel, Health and Fitness Club.

If you would like further details, please don't hesitate to contact me at (514) 989-7299.

Sincerely,

Paul Kubecki

Commendation Letter: Sample 3 (teacher)

(Commendation from a private citizen normally printed on standard stationery)

45 Muskoka Drive West
Orillia, ON
L3V 7T5

August 28, 2002

Ms. Patricia Morton
Couchiching District Secondary School
78 Andrew St. S.
Orillia, ON
L4S 3R2

Dear Ms. Morton:

The purpose of this is to thank you for the positive influence you have had on our daughter Samantha this past school year.

Up until this year, Samantha had problems every year with her English language studies. This year we have noticed a dramatic turnaround, and it is clear to us that it is directly attributable to your teaching methods. Samantha's average in English Language Studies is now in the mid 80s when in previous years, she has never received an average over 65% in those subjects.

It also shows in Samantha's general attitude towards all of her subjects, and school in general. For the first time that we can remember, she looks forward to going to school and to your English Literature and Drama classes in particular. Her overall average for all subjects has increased this year by over 10 points, to above 80%.

Veronica and I feel that the changes in Samantha's attitude and marks have been so dramatic that we wanted to formally thank you for your efforts on our daughter's behalf. We have also taken the liberty of sending a copy of this letter to your Principal, Jackson Davies.

Thank you so much for what you have done for our daughter.

Yours sincerely,

Patrick and Veronica Miller

cc: Mr. Jackon Davies
        Principal, Couchiching District Secondary School

Commendation Letter: Sample 4 (award)

(Award Commendation normally printed on corporate memo letterhead stationery)

CONFIDENTIAL MEMORANDUM

Date: September 12, 2002

From: Peter Hartley

To: Ken Handler
             Executive Director

Subject: <u>Nomination – Barbara Meltzer– Roderick Shore Award, 2002</u>

The purpose of this is to submit the name of Barbara Meltzer as a nominee for the 2002 "Roderick Shore Award for Excellence in Aircraft Accident Investigation."

Since July 1998 when Barbara first joined this agency, she has consistently demonstrated her superior skills, abilities, and professionalism as a member of the aviation accident investigation group. I believe that she is a shining example of everything that is signified by the "Roderick Shore Award", and she should be given the award for 2002. I will briefly summarize my reasons for my nomination:

- Barbara was instrumental in leading a successful search and recovery effort when the Air Orion B-707 crashed into Lake Ontario in December 2000.

- As investigator-in-charge of the Air Orion investigation, she has set a new standard for applying project management techniques to a major accident investigation.

- Barbara's performance in dealing with all parties involved has been exceptional. These parties included: next-of-kin, the media, police forces, interested parties, and other government agencies. She is clearly a gifted communicator and negotiator.

- She and her team of investigators managed to produce a comprehensive draft report for Board review within 15 months of the accident date. As you know, this is unprecedented for a major investigation and has set a new standard for this agency.

- Even though she was pre-occupied with the Air Orion investigation, Barbara managed to make significant contributions to the drafting of the Board's new "Investigation Policy".

I'm sure you will agree that Barbara's contribution has been outstanding and exemplifies the qualities of excellence, and professionalism that are embodied in the Roderick Shore Award.

I look forward to our discussion of nominees at next week's Management Council Meeting.

Peter Hartley
Director, Investigation Operations

Commendation Letter: Sample 5 (community service)

(Commendation from a private citizen normally printed on standard stationery)

435 Fourth Ave.
Ann Arbor, MI
49637

October 15, 2002

Mr. Albert Wolfson
Executive Director
Citizen's Volunteer Center
748 Center Street
Ann Arbor, MI, 49652

Dear Mr. Wolfson:

I am writing this to you on the advice of the Mayor's Office. My initial inclination was to write there but when I called, they told me to send my letter to you.

The purpose of this letter is to inform you of one of our citizens who I believe should receive some special recognition for dedicated community service. The person to whom I refer is Elizabeth Samuelson. I believe you know Elizabeth in your position as volunteer coordinator.

I have known Elizabeth for more than 20 years as both a friend and a neighbor. During that time I have seen her work tirelessly on scores of community projects and committees. As far as I know, she has never received any kind of recognition from the community for her work. I believe she should be given some sort of special recognition.

Just last year alone, she worked on at least six different community projects including the Park Renewal Project, and the Heritage Homes Fund-Raising Banquet. I believe she is also a member of a number of ongoing committees including the Library Restoration Committee and the Citizens for Literacy Committee. In addition, she is a weekly driver for the Meals-on-Wheels program and she visits patients at the palliative care unit at the hospital on a regular basis.

I'm sure that if you check with a few of your staff members who have been there over the years, they will confirm Elizabeth's community service record and probably be able to add many examples to the few I have given here. (By the way, Elizabeth has no idea that I am writing this. She is a low-key, humble person, and if she were aware of it, she would not allow me to send it.)

I have thought about writing such a letter about Elizabeth a number of times in the past but just never took action. Then last week, I noticed in the paper that you sponsor an annual dinner at which dozens of awards are given out to people with much less community service than Elizabeth. In fact, I checked with her and she has never even been invited to that annual event!

I urge you to correct that omission now and take action to see that Elizabeth Samuelson is properly recognized for her many years of silent but outstanding service to this community.

Yours truly,

Linda Sullivan

cc: Office of Mayor John Everest

PERFORMANCE EVALUATION LETTERS

In general, these are usually detailed assessments of an employee's work performance as part of an organization's regular employee review process. Typically, they are written by the employee's supervisor and are attached to the individual's performance appraisal and placed on their personnel file.

The format and structure for this type of letter is more often than not dictated by the "employee performance evaluation system" or process that is in-place where the subject of the letter is employed.

It should be noted that not all employers require a "performance evaluation letter." In fact, in recent years the vast majority of employers have developed their own internal performance appraisal systems.

These systems usually make use of fixed pre-formatted performance appraisal "checklist" forms that break a person's job performance down into six to eight performance areas, or factors. Narrative is kept to a minimum and there is no requirement for a "performance evaluation letter."

Nevertheless, the use of "performance evaluation letters" is still quite widespread in the academic community. Accordingly, this section of the guide is primarily focused on the evaluation letters related to the field of academia, particularly at the college and university levels.

DRAFTING TIPS – EVALUATION LETTERS

For general letter writing tips please refer back to the section earlier in this guide titled "Letter Writing Guidelines."

Following are some tips to keep in mind when drafting a performance evaluation letter about someone:

Stick To The Facts

Limit your comments to specifics, and avoid subjective statements without supplying substantiation. It is not good enough to simply say "Professor

Sample's classroom was sub-standard". You need to substantiate such a statement with some facts or specific examples.

For example, "As evidenced by student evaluations, classroom audits, and review of teaching materials, in my judgment Professor Sample's classroom teaching falls short of the standard of professionalism expected in this department".

If you can't substantiate with some corroborating evidence, you're better off to not make the statement at all. If there is an area of weakness, but you can't really prove it, take measures to document it during the next session so that you can deal with it in the next performance evaluation.

Try To Keep It Short

There can be a tendency to go on and on when writing one of these letters, forever explaining and qualifying the points that are being made. Repetition is redundant in a performance evaluation letter, unless what is being repeated makes a completely different point. In general, make a particular point once, in a clear and concise manner, and then move on.

Watch Your Language

Word choice is particularly important when writing performance evaluation letters. People tend to take these letters personally! After the letter is written, you will have to discuss it with the person being evaluated. Later it will be seen by other people during the performance review process, and it will end up on the employee's personnel file.

Choose objective, neutral words and phrases. Avoid anything that is emotionally-charged in any way. If someone is a satisfactory performer, but you personally can't stand the person for some reason, keep this latter point out of the evaluation letter.

Keep It Confidential

Because of their highly personal nature, performance evaluation letters should always be kept confidential during all stages of the drafting process. Only those people directly involved in the process should ever see one.

SAMPLE TEMPLATES - EVALUATION LETTERS

The following pages contain fully-formatted real-life performance evaluation letter templates written for various real-life working situations.

Although the templates included here relate to the academic field, the approaches and phraseology can be applied in any situation where a formal performance evaluation letter is required.

Evaluation Letter: Sample 1 (satisfactory)

(Performance Evaluation Letter is normally printed on corporate letterhead stationery)

CONFIDENTIAL

April 10, 2002

Professor Ralph Hewson
P.O. Box 9010
Postal Station UNI
Michigan Ave. West
Chicago, IL, 60601

Dear Professor Hewson:

This performance evaluation letter covers your performance as a tenured associate professor from April 1, 2001 to March 31, 2002. This evaluation focuses on three major areas weighted as follows: teaching (65%), research (25%) and service (10%). It also takes into consideration your responsibilities and obligations as a faculty member.

Teaching
Your teaching performance has been evaluated as average by both your peers and students. Based on my observations of your teaching methods and instructional materials during my periodic audits, I agree with that assessment. This average rating is partially offset by the great success you have achieved in developing a reputation as a preferred advisor. I congratulate you on your success in this area. In addition, you deserve the appreciation of the entire faculty for doing the lion's share of the work in preparing the instructional materials for the new first-year mandatory courses.

Research
I note that the majority of your research activities are directly related to new communication techniques and technology. I am also aware that two of your articles were published this past year by a very prestigious journal in the academic communications field. You have also presented a number of excellent papers on this subject. The CanComm Award that you received last year continues to give you many opportunities to showcase your work. It also reflects well on the department and the school as a whole.

In the coming year, I urge you to continue to submit papers to refereed publications and to continue to build up your dossier in your own field, rather than focusing solely on communications technology. Overall, I find your performance in research to be above average.

Services
In general, your governance and service activities continue to be satisfactory, and consistent with your departmental assignments. However, I have noticed a decline in this area during the past year, when compared with previous years. Your level of participation has fallen off and you avoid commencing new initiatiatives. I encourage you to get more involved. I suggest you accept the chair of the search committee as we try to fill the three vacant positions in the department. This would be an excellent concrete demonstration of your commitment to the service aspect of your position.

Overall
In summary, for reasons indicated in the foregoing, I have assessed your overall performance this past year to be satisfactory, but with improvements needed. I would like to see you focus more on diversity in both your instructional program and in your research endeavors. I encourage you to make a point to observe some of your colleagues in action and see how they conduct classes and keep the students engaged. As noted, I expect you to take a pro-active role in filling the vacant positions in the department.

In closing, I am pleased to recommend your appointment for the coming academic year. Your provisional schedule for next year is attached to this.

I would ask you to please sign and date this letter where indicated below after we have had our discussion on its contents.

Sincerely,

Agnes Ledbetter, Ph.D.
Department Head

By my signature, I acknowledge having discussed or reviewed the above letter of evaluation. I have __ have not __ attached additional comments with the intent that they become a part of my personnel file.

_____
Signature of Person Evaluated

cc: Dean M. Hughes
        Personnel File – R. Hewson

Evaluation Letter: Sample 2 (excellent)

(Performance Evaluation Letter is normally printed on corporate letterhead stationery)

CONFIDENTIAL

April 30, 2002

Professor Marilyn Chang
Performing Arts Center
Lakeview Campus
Berkeley, CA, 94705

Dear Professor Chang:

This letter constitutes the formal written evaluation of your assigned duties and professional responsibilities for the past academic year. This review is based on: your performance of assigned and associated duties and responsibilities, reviews of recent creative works you have completed, results of the Tenure Assessment Committee's annual review of the student teaching evaluation results, and on my own review and observations of your assigned and related duties and responsibilities. The three areas of evaluation are: teaching (80%), creative activity (15%), and services and administration (5%).

PERFORMANCE EVALUATION

Teaching and Instruction (80%)
As in previous years, your teaching continues to be excellent, both in the classroom and in the performance studio. Members of the Tenure Assessment Committee who have observed you in action have noted that you devote a great deal of personal effort and interest to your daily teaching activities, and to your students. Not surprisingly, student evaluations of your teaching are very high in all categories rated. I have noted that you continue to be open and receptive to suggestions as to how your teaching can grow and improve. I am impressed by the ways in which you have responded positively to some of the suggestions made during our previous annual reviews. You continue to make an outstanding contribution to the teaching and instructional program of this department.

I note that in addition to your assigned teaching responsibilities, you serve regularly on a number of committees, and frequently present master classes at other institutions. Your colleagues find you to be frank and direct in discussions but always ready to listen to new and/or different ideas.

Creative Activities (15%)
Your creative achievements remain excellent in every respect. In the past year, you have participated in numerous faculty performances on campus and in the community. Your recital performances are regarded as excellent, both within the state and across the country. You have also been invited to participate in an international concert tour in recognition of your excellence.

In addition to your performing, you have also achieved excellent success as a composer. Your compositions include six commissioned pieces, as well as three other published works. I am especially pleased that your work is frequently performed by orchestras in both this country and abroad. This is an amazing accomplishment for someone in an early teaching career and reflects very favorably on the department and the university.

Services and Administration (5%)
You continue to be involved in departmental management through your work on the University's Equal Opportunities Committee and your participation on the New Talent Search Committee. Additional service activities include your participation in a department-sponsored seminar, a performance festival, your service on the Board of Directors of the Berkeley Symphony Orchestra,

and your continued performance as a member of the Valley Youth Orchestra. I believe that your level of involvement in these various activities is outstanding.

You have now completed your second year of tenure-earning status. I find that your overall performance in all three areas of teaching, creative achievements, and services/administration continue to be excellent, and completely consistent with your assignment.

PROGRESS TOWARD TENURE

The excellent quality of your work has been recognized and commended once again by the members of the Tenure Assessment Committee. You continue to achieve distinction, both on and off campus as noted in reviews and comments made by your colleagues and others. I note that you continually strive for improvement in all areas of endeavor. You are well-liked and respected by your colleagues. Your ability to respond positively to constructive suggestions and learn from them is exceptional. I encourage you to continue with your efforts in all of these areas.

As you enter your third year of tenure-earning status, I would like to suggest some ways in which you should continue to strive for continued growth:

- Focus on being more selective and discerning in the types and number of professional and creative activities that you engage in. Your shift in focus to more off-campus and regional activities last year had a positive impact and was wise. I suggest you prioritize a little more, in order to give yourself more balance and flexibility.

- Work on improving your awareness relative to how others view you in professional settings. Make sure that your interaction with colleagues will lead toward the accomplishment of your professional goals.

- Continue with your program to strengthen and expand your studio workshop series. The current enrolment of twelve students for next year looks promising.

- Continue on your path of composing and performing in ways that bring credit to you, the department, and the university.

- You should continue to refine your comprehensive teaching portfolio, which will be key in presenting a thorough profile of your teaching work when you apply for tenure and promotion.

- Continue to explore creative ways in which to develop new instructional materials for your classes, particularly for working with students of varying learning styles.

In summary, you continue to make wonderful contributions to our faculty and the department as a whole, and I regard myself as fortunate to be your colleague. Your hard work and exceptional commitment and dedication are appreciated by all whom know you. Accordingly, I am pleased to recommend that you be reappointed as Assistant Professor for the 2002-03 academic year. Have a great summer and take some time for yourself!

The following is a list of your primary duties and responsibilities (scheduled and non-scheduled) for the 2002-03 academic year. The list includes those other duties and responsibilities attendant to being a faculty member. Please note that due to the unpredictability of final student registration, your actual responsibilities during the coming year could be somewhat different from these. We often have to make adjustments in assignments after the teaching year has begun.

Teaching/Instructional Activities - 2002-03 (provisional)
Performance Studio and Studio Workshop
Academic Classes in Music Theory
Composition Review and Critiques
Projects and Courses as needed
Thursday Afternoon Auditions
Faculty Meetings

Creative Activities and Services
In addition to teaching and instructional activities, it is expected that each member of the faculty shall engage in creative activities such as performance, composition, and research appropriate to the person's position. A form will be provided at the late-August faculty meeting, to be used for submitting a written statement of your plans for performances, research or other creative activities for the academic year 2002-03.

Please review the draft of your annual performance evaluation letter and sign it the bottom where indicated if you accept the evaluation. You may attach any comments you might have for the record and return them to me no later than next Monday. If you disagree with the evaluation and/or would like to meet with me to discuss it or related matters, please make an appointment with me as soon as possible.

Sincerely,

Boris Kafelnekov, Ph.D.
Department Chair

_____
Faculty Member's Signature/Date

cc: Dean R. Gustafson
    Personnel File - M. Chang

Evaluation Letter: Sample 3 (borderline)

(Performance Evaluation Letter is normally printed on corporate letterhead stationery)

CONFIDENTIAL

November 25, 2002

Professor Ronald Bates
Arts Complex
UniCenter, Box 4250
Calgary, AB, T2E 5Y7

Dear Professor Bates:

This letter serves as the annual written evaluation of your assigned and related duties for this academic year at this University. It has been prepared in compliance with Article 43.7 of the directives of the University Board of Governors.

The evaluation of activity areas is weighted as follows: teaching (60%), research (30%), public service and administartion (10%).

Teaching and Instruction (60%)
Your teaching assignment for the past year (60%) involved courses at the undergraduate and graduate levels. You also served on three Masters committees (two as chair), and on three Doctoral Committees (one as chair).

As we discussed during our recent annual review meeting, I am quite concerned about a number of things that have transpired in some of your classes. These concerns have been reflected in low student ratings, and in complaints from students about your teaching practices. This is almost exactly the same situation that existed one year ago. There has been little or no improvement since then. These complaints have also been brought to my attention on several occasions this past year by graduate students. They include the following:

- You do not create a focused and orderly atmosphere in your classes. This is reflected by the absence of continuity and consistency in your class lectures. The haphazard way in which you follow up with students on their homework assignments has also been criticized. As I pointed out last year, and on a number of occasions in the past few months, you need to focus more and organize your teaching approach.

- Your classes frequently do not begin on time and you do not provide appropriate instructional materials. These concerns were strongly reflected in student evaluations. I raised these points with you in your annual review last year, as well as in a series of conversations we had since the winter study break.

- You do not regularly attend academic meetings during which matters relating to the continuity of the academic program and related issues are discussed and decided upon. Numerous of your colleagues have stated that, when you do attend, you tend to be negative and are not particularly collegial in your interactions.

- You do not provide regular and consistent formal assessments and feedback to students about their progress and how they can work toward improvement.

- Your overall failure to perform your duties properly is clearly evidenced in the low student ratings of your teaching performance over the past year. Your ratings in all of your fall-term courses were extremely low. In the "Overall" category, yours were among the lowest of all faculty ratings during the same period.

With reference to the foregoing, and as we discussed when we met recently, I consider your teaching performance to be unsatisfactory. Accordingly, I must formally advise you now that if I do not see significant improvement in the areas discussed in this letter over the coming year I will have no choice but to but to take the actions I discussed with you.

I strongly urge you to contact the Department of Instructional Support for assistance in analyzing some of your lectures. In addition, I plan to visit your classes unannounced on at least three occasions during the coming winter and spring terms. My observations, coupled with your own analysis, should give you plenty of ways to improve your classroom teaching and demeanor. You might also want to ask one or two of your senior colleagues to observe you in the classroom and to provide you with constructive feedback which you can put into action.

Research And Scholarly Achievements (30%)
You have made several achievements in the area of research and scholarship (30%) over the past year. Most notable was the publication of your research in one article in a refereed journal, and your presentation of same, at a national conference. However, I find this level of productivity to be marginal considering your status as a Full Professor.

I expect you to increase your research and scholarly output significantly during the coming year. If your output in this area does not increase to my satisfaction, the percentage of time assigned for research next year will be decreased and an additional course will be added to your teaching load in future terms.

Public Service and Administration (10%)
Your public service and departmental administrative activities (10%) were borderline satisfactory over the past year. These included limited contributions and sporadic participation on the Departmental Library Acquisitions Committee. In addition, you participated in only 60% of the sessions of the International Scholarship Review Committee. I would also expect you to be more active in one or more of the professional organizations related to your specialty discipline.

It has come to my attention that, in addition to your specific assigned duties, you have also been involved in activities outside of the University that could be deemed in conflict. For example, your extensive consulting activities which were never reported and reviewed in accordance with the University's conflict of interest policy, appear to be in blatant conflict to the guidelines.

In light of the foregoing assessment of your academic and related activities as a faculty member, I find your overall performance over the past academic year to be unsatisfactory and in need of significant improvement.

Following are your assignments for the Winter and Spring Semesters:

- Three (3) Academic Courses – Please note that due to the unpredictability of final student enrollment, your actual assigned responsibilities during the coming year could be somewhat different from the above. It is often necessary to make adjustments in assignments after the year has begun.

- Departmental Committees as elected/assigned during the session.

- Advising students as required.

In addition to teaching and related activities, it is expected that each member of the faculty will engage in: research and scholarly activities appropriate for the individual's position, service to the Department and/or University, and performance of those other duties and responsibilities normally expected of a member of the academic teaching staff.

If you agree with this evaluation, please sign and date it where indicated and return it to my office by this Friday. If you disagree with this evaluation and/or would like to meet with me to discuss it, please make an appointment with me as soon as possible.

Sincerely,

Brian Jamieson, Ph.D., MSc.
Department Chair

By my signature, I acknowledge having discussed the above letter of evaluation and request ___ /do not request ___ that the attached comments be filed with this letter in my personnel file.

_____
Signature of Professor Evaluated/Date

cc: Dean Z. Ayoub
        Personnel file – R. Bates

Evaluation Letter: Sample 4 (unsatisfactory)

(Performance Evaluation Letter is normally printed on corporate letterhead stationery)

CONFIDENTIAL

August 20, 2002

Professor Judith Weiser
Campus Learning Center
1500 Heritage Circle
Cincinatti, OH, 45201

Dear Professor Weiser:

This letter is a draft of my evaluation of your annual and sustained performance as a tenured full-professor. The evaluations focus on your three major areas of assignment: teaching/instruction (60%), research (30%) and service (10%), as well as on other related duties and responsibilities pertinent to your position at the University.

ANNUAL EVALUATION

Teaching and Instruction (60%)
As evidenced by my review of your teaching and instructional material and the results of your fall student evaluations, your teaching continues to be of superior quality. You have maintained a reputation as one of our most popular and effective teachers. Your involvement in teaching those difficult beginning level undergraduate courses is appreciated. You have also performed well in your other teaching-related activities and assignments, including your development of unique new teaching methods and aids.

Although your teaching evaluations remain above average, there has been a spate of recent complaints from a number of students about your conduct in the classroom, i.e. short-tempered behavior, use of inappropriate language, tardiness, being preoccupied, and not being prepared for class. We discussed these issues recently and you have indicated that you understand the concerns and will address them.

Research (30%)
Your activities for the past year in grant-funded research have been very disappointing. I realize that because a few of your graduate students are completing their work, it has been a busy time for you. Nevertheless, by failing to provide the required grant reports when required, you have missed the opportunity to have your current grant considered for continuation. Furthermore, you have not submitted any other grant proposals. Consequently there is no support for your graduate students. In addition, your publication activities have virtually ground to a halt. For these reasons, I consider you performance in your research to be unsatisfactory this year.

Service and Other (10%)
Your performance with respect to your normal departmental professional duties appears to also be at a standstill. Your attendance record at department committee and faculty meetings and seminars is spotty at best. It seems that in recent months you have almost isolated yourself from your colleagues and from the normal professional activities of the department. When you do occasionally attend, you appear to be confrontational rather than positive and productive. A number of your colleagues have expressed concern about this relatively sudden change in your demeanor. As I mentioned, in the previous section many of your students have also complained about your temper and sudden outbursts. We discussed this recently and you assured me that although you have recently experienced some personal problems, things are now under control.

Overall, with the exception of your classroom teaching, I believe your performance of the responsibilities to you as a faculty member are less than satisfactory this year, particularly the most recent term. This last period certainly does not reflect your normal performance. In summary, based on your annual report, student evaluations, peer reviews, and my own observations, it is my view that your overall performance is below average and in need of immediate and significant improvement.

SUSTAINED PERFORMANCE EVALUATION

With respect to your sustained performance over the past six (6) years, I find your overall performance to be satisfactory, excluding this past year. Your classroom work has always been your major strength, and I continue to view it as excellent. Prior to this past year, your research activities were always excellent. I realize that you have had some personal challenges and problems recently, which have degraded your performance. You have indicated that you are taking action on these and expect things to improve in the near future. As we discussed, in order to give you time to regroup, your classroom teaching assignment will be reduced this year. This will give you some extra time for course preparation, to conduct library research, and to revitalize your research program. We also discussed the possibility of you utilizing some of the on-campus resources such as life management counseling to help you deal with some of the problems you face. I trust you will avail of some of these programs during the coming year.

Please regard this as notification of your reappointment for the next academic year. Your tentative teaching assignments for next year will be two sections per term of your regular course in Literary Classics (50%). Your research assignment will be increased to 45% to give you more time to conduct research and develop and submit grant applications. In addition, your normal service component will be reduced (5%). As we discussed, I am hoping that you will also agree to chair two proposal review committees, as well as serve on the scholarship review committee. In addition to these assigned duties, you are responsible for other duties and responsibilities normally expected from a member of the faculty that are related to your employment at the university.

If you agree with this evaluation, please sign and date it where indicated and return it to my office by next Monday. If you disagree with it and/or would like to meet with me to discuss it, please make an appointment with me for early next week.

I wish you success in the coming year. Please let me know if I can assist you in any way.

Sincerely,

Marisa Thomasino, Ph.D.
Department Chair

By my signature I acknowledge having discussed the above letter of evaluation and request ___ do not request ___ that the attached comments be filed with this letter in my personnel file.

_____
Faculty member's signature/Date

cc:	Dean L. Rassmussen
	Personnel File – J. Weiser

Evaluation Letter: Sample 5 (request for letter)

(Performance Evaluation Letter Request is normally printed on corporate letterhead stationery)

November 24, 2002

Dr. Simon Braithwaite
Professor, English Literature Studies
Department of English Literature
Arts and Sciences Building
7500 Edgewater Way
Portland, OR, 97213

Dear Professor Braithwaite:

I would like to thank you in advance for agreeing to draft a letter of evaluation for the tenure of Dr. Purie to the position of Full Professor in my department. To guide us in evaluating Dr. Purie's professional performance, we are seeking your considerd opinions as to the quality of the contributions that he has made in his field.

There are a number of factors that will be taken into consideration when deciding whether Dr. Purie should be promoted at this time. Although crucial to our evaluation, your input will be one of a number, so our decision will not be made on your input alone. We have contacted you as expert in Dr. Purie's field and ask you to please limit your comments to issues related specifically to your professional discipline. Here are the specific aspects that we would like you to address:

1. Provide background as to how long, and in what capacity you have known the candidate.

2. Your professional opinion as to the the quality, originality, and significance of the candidate's published works, with emphasis on the more recent work.

3. Your overall assessment of the candidate's national and international standing relative to other outstanding individuals in the same field at a similar stage of development.

Enclosed, you will find copies of various documents relative to your review. I realize that your review of these will be somewhat time-consuming. Nevertheless, I am sure that you are fully aware of the need for such rigorous assessments in order to maintain standards in the field.

During the evaluation process, your letter will be kept on a confidential file only available to members of the Evaluation Committee and limited academic support and administrative staff. However, as in most jurisdictions, the law requires that at the end of the review process the letter must be placed on the candidates's confidential personnel file, which will be available to him.

The Committee requires your letter of evaluation of Dr. Purie by January 15, 2003.

On behalf of the university and the faculty of this department, I sincerely thank you for giving your professional time to this important matter. Don't hesitate to call me at (503) 287-5378 should you have any questions.

Sincerely,

Gerald Otterson, Ph.D.

enclosures

BONUS SECTION!

COLLEGE ADMISSION ESSAYS

This guide wouldn't be complete in covering recommendation letters related to college and university admission without also addressing one of the most critical documents that must also accompany the application for admission – the college admission essay.

As entry into college and university programs becomes increasingly competitive, the importance of a well-written admission essay or essay set cannot be over-emphasized. These essays are normally required for consideration for admission into both the graduate and undergraduate programs, although the specific requirements may vary at each level.

Aside from the standard academic performance metrics, these admission essays are the one chance that a student has to show who they are, what they've done, and how they can express themselves. They go beyond the actual academic achievement to show a little bit about the actual "person" behind the application.

It's a chance for the student to show their human side to the officials that review admission applications.

ADMISSION ESSAY TERMINOLOGY AND REQUIREMENTS

The terminology used to describe these documents can be very confusing at times. My research has revealed that there are a number of different terms that are widely used to signify the generic "college admission essay." These terms vary from country to country, and often from school to school within the same country.

Here is a list of the most common terms that are used to describe the "college admission essay":

- Admission essay

- College essay
- Graduate admission essay
- Personal statement
- Statement of purpose

Specific requirements for what must go into the admission essay will vary for college to college. Sometimes, the requirement will be to write a one to two page essay on the topic of your choice. Other times, you may be asked to choose an essay topic from a list of pre-specified topics.

A common approach is to ask an applicant to write an essay that answers a specific question. For example, the question could be "Define your five (5) most dominant personality characteristics and describe how they will affect your future academic and professional careers?".

In most cases, unless otherwise stated, your resume should range in length somewhere between 600 and 800 words (about a page and a half, single spaced).

A few universities may even require you to write a set of short essays on a list of pre-selected topics (e.g. Harvard).

Regardless of the specific requirements at a particular university or college, the overall approach to writing an admission essay is essentially the same.

ADMISSION ESSAY REVIEW PROCESS

Typically, the admission review process involves three levels of review: admission assistants, associate directors of admission, and the director of admissions.

Your application and essay will be reviewed first by the admission assistants. These people are normally recent graduates, perhaps four or five years older than you. If they like your essay, they will recommend it for further review at the next higher level.

The next level is the associate admissions officer. These are normally career employees at the college or university who have spent many years reviewing admission submissions and essays. If the associate admissions person likes your essay, they will pass it up the ladder to the Director of Admissions who will make the final decision.

Together, these three levels are often referred to as the "Admissions Committee."

Most colleges and universities receive thousands of applications beyond the number of students that they can admit in any given year. This relatively small admissions review group must review each and every application and read each and every essay for applicants that meet the minimum admission requirements.

Needless to say, during peak periods these people are overloaded with work and often have to read dozens of essays in one day.

This is why it is so important that you write an admission essay that stands out from the crowd. Your essay must grab the reviewer's attention in the opening paragraph. It must draw them in and interest them at once, and convince them to move your file on the pile designated "for further review" that will go to the next level.

If your essay makes it to the Director of Admissions level, there is a very good chance that your application for admission will be accepted.

WHAT THEY'RE LOOKING FOR

It's not just about the marks.

The people on the Admissions Committee are not looking for more than evidence of your academic achievements. Enough of that type of information is already included in the other sections of your application.

Colleges and universities are not just looking for academic geniuses these days. As society and the world change, these institutions are also seeking people with diverse backgrounds, experiences, and interests. They are interested in people who will make unique contributions to university life, and eventually to society in general.

Your admission essay allows you to show another dimension of yourself that may not come across clearly in the rest of your application.

It's about you, the human being. The essay can highlight your personal strengths and unique personal characteristics and show you as a balanced and well-rounded individual, rather than just an academic achiever.

Don't underestimate the importance of the essay. All other things being equal, it is the essay that will determine whether you get accepted, or not.

DRAFTING TIPS – COLLEGE ADMISSION ESSAYS

As mentioned above, the specific requirements for essays will vary from school to school. However, the general approach and the basics for writing a good admission essay are essentially the same.

The following are a number of key tips that will help you draft a better college admission essay:

Make It A Personal Statement

The admissions committee isn't looking for bureaucratic bafflegab or pie-in-the-sky platitudes. They want to know a little bit more about you, the person, the human being. Who exactly are you? What makes you unique? How do you see the world? What do you have to offer as a person? What will you bring to the academic and social life at the university? The general essay requirements and the questions are designed to elicit this kind of information from you. Make sure you don't blow this opportunity.

Here's an important word of caution. Don't forget that the overall purpose of the essay is for the readers to get to know you in the broader sense. Make sure your essay doesn't focus exclusively on one aspect of your personality or one life-changing event. Make sure you paint the bigger picture of you.

Write It For The Committee

When you are planning and writing your essay keep in mind at all times who will be reading it – the Admissions Committee. Try to picture these people in your mind's eye as you write. What would they expect? What kind of information will they be looking for? Are you presenting the material appropriately for this audience?

To get a better "feel" for the Admissions Committee it can be helpful to go to the school's Web site and spend some time in the Admissions area, seeing how they are organized, and viewing the names and qualifications of the staff listed there. This can make it easier to visualize the committee as you write your essay.

Keep The Language and Structure Simple

The most effective approach is to write the essay as you would speak. Imagine yourself sitting across a boardroom table from three of four members of the Admissions Committee. Write your essay just as you would speak in that situation – simple, direct, clear. Keep the paragraphs and sentences short. Breaking your essay into three or four sentence paragraphs will make it more pleasing to the eye and easier to scan.

As an editor, I can tell you that there is nothing worse than having to work on a dense page of run-on sentences with few paragraph breaks. You just don't want to go on reading. If you have good content, don't turn your readers off with poor sentence or paragraph structure.

Don't Repeat What They Already Know

Make sure that your essay doesn't just reiterate information that is already included in other parts of your application package. For example, don't spend time going over your academic achievements when they are covered in another specific part of the application.

For your essay, choose a topic or an angle that presents different information about you that can't be found elsewhere in the application.

Answer The Question

Many college admission applications will ask you to answer a specific question. Questions such as: "Describe a significant childhood experience and how that shaped you into the person you are today." Or, "Describe the one or two individuals who have influenced you thus far in your life and explain how that influence has changed and/or guided you."

If you get one of these questions, be sure that you answer it directly and specifically. When you are at the final draft stage it's a good idea to go back to the original question and make sure that you have answered it properly and completely.

Sometimes the question will be much more open-ended, such as, "Describe your personal characteristics and explain how they prepare you for admission into this program." Even with a broader question like this, it is easy to get off-course.

Don't write your essay about a tragedy in the family unless you tie it directly into how it shaped you into a prime candidate for the program to which you are applying.

Don't Try To Be Too Cute

Don't take your essay too lightly. Remember, these admissions committee people are faced with making difficult decisions that impact people's lives. A sense of humor can be great and there is nothing wrong with showing this side of your personality in your essay. Just don't go overboard. The readers of your essay are being asked to make a serious decision that will change your life. They need some serious straightforward material to do that.

Also, be careful using humor. A sense of humor is a very individualized attribute. What may be hilarious to one person can fall flat with another.

Target The School If Possible

Your ability to do this will vary depending on the specific form of your essay and/or the wording of your question. However, if you possibly can, weave the target school into your essay. First, go to the school's Web site. Take a look at the opening pages that give the general information about the school you are applying to. Look for statements like: mission, vision, guiding principles, educational priorities, etc. Letters from senior faculty members are often good sources of material for this.

If you read this material carefully you will spot certain words, phrases and/or ideas popping up again and again. These are the signposts of the institutional culture of that college or university. If you can possibly slant your essay to incorporate one or more of these themes, it will definitely add value to your submission.

For example, say that one of the overriding themes of the college you are researching is, for example, "… social and cultural diversity for the new millennium." See if you can find something about you or your experiences that ties into this theme. Perhaps you are from another culture. Or, maybe you have traveled widely or lived abroad and therefore have a better than average understanding of other cultures.

This is just an example. If you look carefully and think about it, there are probably a number of these or similar themes that you could relate to in your essay.

Focus On Your Uniqueness

You want your essay to somehow make you stand out among hundreds of others. To do this, your essay must be different. The essay itself can use a different approach (which can sometimes be risky) and/or it can highlight something particularly unique about you.

Think about what unusual experiences, interests, and/or hobbies you might have. Try to weave one or more of these into your essay in an interesting way. Think hard. Everyone has some unique and/or unusual characteristics and/or interests that make then stand out from their peers in some way.

You don't have to be a child prodigy who became a concert pianist to be unique. Maybe you have an impressive butterfly collection, or you are addicted to golf. Working these into your essay in an interesting and positive way will help your essay.

Tell A Story Of Personal Change and Growth

Essays that tell a story of how you have changed in a positive way due to one or more events in your life can be very effective. Or, it might have been another person who influenced you to change. Simply, describe that event and/or person and explain how it changed you for the better. A story of how you faced a personal problem or challenge and managed to overcome it, and how that changed you to become a better person can make for a powerful essay.

But, be careful to make sure that your essay is focused on you, and how you changed, and not on the life-changing event or person.

Write About You and What You Know

Sometimes there is a tendency to write beyond one's personal experience and knowledge in order to impress, or meet perceived expectations. This is never effective, and can almost always be recognized by experienced readers. Stick to what you know, what you've experienced, and where you have been. A simple story can still make a good essay if approached properly and written well.

Most importantly, be honest and be yourself. Don't try to invent a new you. Living a lie is just not worth it. If you did manage by some small miracle to get through the admissions committee without being identified as a fraud, it would just be a matter of time. Eventually you will get caught and be exposed, and then everything that you have accomplished up until that time will be in jeopardy.

Avoid Controversial Subjects

Your college admission essay is not the time to get up on the soapbox and try to convert people to your point of view. Members of the admission committee are from all kinds of backgrounds and socio-economic groups.

So, regardless of your personal beliefs in certain sensitive areas, do not write on a subject that might offend one or more of these people. If you do, you will be shooting yourself in the foot. Doing this will definitely not help you get accepted into the college or university of your choice.

Specifically, avoid writing about politics, religion, or controversial issues such as the legalization of marijuana, abortion, and euthanasia.

Provide Supporting Details

To make your essay interesting and to give it more credibility, make sure that you provide supporting details. Involve the reader using colors, smells, visual descriptions, and feelings. Show that you've "been there and done that." This will engage the reader and will make them relate to you more as a real person, as opposed to just reading neutral, non-involving words on a page.

For example, the sentence "I can still smell the sandalwood smoke that greeted me when I stepped off the airplane at 2:00 a.m. in Bombay" will have more impact than "We arrived in Bombay by plane at 2:00 a.m."
Remember, you're telling a story.

Draft and Then Re-Draft

A good essay should go through at least three or four drafts. This is all part of a natural process that will eventually arrive at a final product. The more time you give yourself to go through this drafting process, the better. If you can do it over a two or three week period, with 3 or 4 day gaps between each draft, that's great. Each time you look at it you will see it from a different perspective until you have fine-tuned it into what you consider a good final draft.

Proof Read and Edit Carefully

Remember that you will be submitting your essay to an academic institution and it will be reviewed by well-educated people with above average writing skills. Accordingly, there is no quicker way to lose your credibility than to submit an admission essay with typos and/or grammatical errors.

Use the spell-checker and grammar checker included with your word processing software. If you don't have one, there are plenty available for free online. Just go to your search engine of choice and enter "free spell checker" or "free grammar checker" to find one.

Remember, although spell-checkers are great, they don't catch everything. For example, I often reverse the letters in certain words when typing quickly. i.e. "form" instead of "from." As far as a spell-checker is concerned, these are both valid words. Some grammar checkers will flag this as being out of context, but you can't always count on that.

The only way to be sure in the end that everything is fine, is to have someone with good spelling and grammar skills do a final check.

Get Feedback From Others

Late in the drafting process, when you are sure of the approach and content and are just in the fine-tuning stages, it is a good idea to ask someone you know and trust to read the essay over and give you their feedback and/or impressions. The two main points you will want to derive from their feedback are whether your essay is an accurate reflection of you, and will the writing stand up? Ideally, this person will be someone who knows you reasonably well and has good writing skills.

In fact, it is a good idea to get a couple of opinions from people with different backgrounds and qualifications who will see the essay from very different perspectives.

Sleep On It One More Time

After you have arrived at the "final draft" of your essay, put it aside and don't think about it, at least for overnight. Even if you aren't thinking about it consciously, your sub-conscious mind will still be working on it. I know this very well from personal experience. Whenever I write something for a client, I try to leave enough time so that I can "sleep on it" and then do one final pass the next day, before I submit it.

No matter how hard I have worked at drafting the document, I invariably find a few final adjustments to make the next day. Without exception, these "adjustments" always improve the final product.

SAMPLE TEMPLATES – COLLEGE ADMISSION ESSAYS

As I mentioned at the beginning of this chapter, the terminology used to describe these admission documents can be somewhat confusing at times.

There are at least five different terms that are commonly used to describe essentially the same thing; the college admission essay. These terms vary from country to country, and sometimes from school to school within the same country.

As already explained, these generic terms for the college admission essay are: admission essay, college essay, graduate admission essay, personal statement, and statement of purpose.

Again, the specific requirements for what must go into the admission essay will vary from college to college. Sometimes, the requirement will be to write a one to two page essay on the topic of your choice. Other times you may be asked to choose an essay topic from a list of pre-specified topics.

Nevertheless, regardless of the specific requirements at a particular university or college, the overall approach to writing an admission essay is essentially the same.

The following pages contain some typical college admission essays. These essays are based on real people in real-life situations but names and specific identifying details have been changed to protect privacy.

Each of the five (5) essays that follows is a response to some of the most common questions asked in college admission applications.

After carefully reviewing these, even if your question(s) is different, you should have a good idea as to how to draft your own essay.

Admission Essay: Sample 1 (life-changing experiences)

Describe one or two significant childhood events that have had a lasting impression on shaping the person you are today.

I'm not sure whether it was that day at the swimming pool when I was 10, or the week that it poured rain when I was 12 that had the biggest impact on the person I have become today. What I do know is that both of those events were important moments of realization for me.

There I was, red-haired, freckle-faced and skinny-white, standing beside the swimming pool with the other boys in my class. All twenty of us were standing there, shoulder-to-shoulder, each one waiting his turn to dive in head-first, swim underwater to the other side of the pool, resurface, and then climb up on the opposite side. That was the simple object of the opening-class-exercise that our burly and gruff male instructor had assigned to us. There was only one problem with this picture. I didn't know how to swim!

But they started anyway. One-by-one, diving in, swimming across the pool, and then jumping up and out. I was second last in line. As I watched the others take their turns, I was filled with fear, wanting to just run up to the instructor and say to him "I can't swim". But for some reason, I just couldn't do that. When my turn finally came, I dove head-first into the water as if I knew exactly what I was doing. Then I proceeded to start drowning. Fortunately, there was a life-saving pole nearby and my instructor managed to fish me out as I choked and spluttered mouthfuls of chlorinated water. Humiliation isn't a powerful enough word to explain what I felt at that moment. Profound shame might be a better description.

This was a clear demonstration as to how far I would already go by the age of 10 years, just to please people. What that incident really boiled down to was the fact that I would choose to look death in the face rather than admit that I couldn't do something. I later realized that I would go to such lengths particularly to please older men, especially if the older man happened to resemble my father in any way. Not surprisingly, the swimming instructor was a younger version of my dad. Why exactly that dynamic existed, is the subject for another essay

But you know what? I did learn to swim that summer. After that incident I somehow managed to screw up my courage, go back to the swimming class, and keep on diving into that water. In that swimming pool, I learned that by facing my fears head-on, I could overcome them.

A couple of years later I was the star pitcher in our suburban baseball league in Dartmouth, Nova Scotia. Near the end of the season the coach asked me if I would like to be the starting pitcher in a special game that had been arranged against the all-star team from the "big city" across the harbor from us. This was a wonderful thing. It was a huge honor, and I had never been so excited about anything before.

The game was to take place the following Saturday. I could hardly wait and had never anticipated something with so much excitement. Saturday came and it was pouring rain. The coach called and said that the game was post-poned to the next day. Sunday came and it was still pouring. The game was re-scheduled for the following Wednesday evening. On Wednesday, it poured all day once again, and the game was re-set for the next Saturday. I believe that we had rain for 30 straight days that summer. It was a record. After Saturday's rain-out I never did hear from that coach again. Somebody said he had gone away on vacation. I felt an empty hole in the pit of my stomach. It stayed right there with me for the rest of that summer, and beyond.

That experience taught me that you can never count on anything for sure. You can plan, and you can prepare, but for the actual event you just have to wait until you get there and see what happens when that day comes.

Now as I seriously contemplate going to college I realize the importance of these two lessons that I learned almost a decade ago. Lesson number one: I can face my fears, and if I do, I will overcome them. Lesson number two: I can do all of the preparation and planning necessary for an event. But I won't worry or obsess about what is going to happen in the future. When the big day comes I'll accept whatever it presents me with.

Admission Essay: Sample 2 (travel and cultural diversity)

Explain how your international travel experiences have affected your view of the world and how they have impacted you as a person?

From as far back as I can remember I have been shuttled back and forth between countries. Later on, it was also between houses, and then finally, between cities. Little did I know at the time, the impact that this living out of a suitcase would have on me as a person, and how it would change my understanding of people, and the world.

My dad and mom met in Canada, were married in India, and then settled back in Canada. After a few years in Canada's capital city, Ottawa, my dad joined a special project team in St. John's, Newfoundland. That's where I was born. So, that makes me a Newfoundlander with an anglo-Canadian father and an indo-Canadian mother. They don't have a name for that combination yet.

After returning to Ottawa, my parents separated and eventually divorced when I was four years old. From that point on, I lived full-time with my mother and stayed with my dad every second weekend, as well as during vacation periods. For a few years, I also stayed with my dad one night each weekday. We did a lot of shuttling back and forth.

Ever since I was a baby I was taken to India by my mother almost every Christmas season to visit my grand parents and cousins. That trip is something I really looked forward to every year. India is such an exciting and exotic place, and I loved visiting my relatives there. Most years, I would leave for India on Boxing Day so that I could also spend time with my dad and his family in Canada on Christmas Eve and Christmas Day.

Once I turned 11 years-old, I was able to fly to India alone and spent most of my summer vacation each year with my grand parents and cousins in New Delhi. Occasionally, I would miss a few days of school in early January because of the India trips. To compensate for this, I would write essays about my experiences in India and in Europe during my travels. I would hand these in as assignments when I got back to school in Ottawa, Sometimes I was even asked to read them to the class.

So, in many ways I have experienced the best of two worlds, India in the East, and Canada in the West. I am fortunate enough to have extended families in both places.

Then, when I was 13 years old my dad moved from small city Ottawa to the big city of Montreal. Since then, I have bused to Montreal every second weekend to see my dad. I have always loved my time in Montreal. It has the feeling of a large vibrant international center that is dripping with multiculturalism and ethnic diversity. I also get to practice my French whenever I'm there.

None of my friends in high school have traveled quite as extensively as I have. Sometimes in class, or even just in casual conversation, I realize how much I have learned in my travels and how they have allowed me to see the "bigger picture" as my dad calls it. I find that my friends sometimes have trouble understanding the differences of other cultures. I know that this is because their only reference point is their own culture. On the other hand, although I don't pretend to know a lot about cultures other than in Canada and India, I think that knowing that there is another dimension leaves me more open to whatever differences another culture may have. I have learned that these differences do exist and must be accepted as they are, with no judgment by one group or the other.

I have no doubt that my multi-cultural background, coupled with my traveling experiences, have created my current interest in pursuing studies in world affairs and international development.

The way I see it, we're all together here, co-existing in our diversity, on this beautiful planet of ours. So, let's just try to be tolerant and accepting and enjoy each other's company. With the proliferation of the Internet and the global economy, the world is quickly becoming a much smaller place than it was during my parent's youth. Before long we're all going to have to learn to get along as one big extended family.

Admission Essay: Sample 3 (targeted university)

Explain why you have chosen to apply for admission ino this particular college (or university)?

I know it sounds a little strange, but I have wanted to go to McGill University ever since I was 10 years old.

I believe I picked up this notion during one of my semi-annual visits to my cousins' place in London, England. Often, during dinner conversation, the adult discussion would turn to where the kids (us) would go to college when they (we) got older. I don't remember much about those conversations except for one thing. Invariably, I would hear the phrase, "… in North America, it has got to be either Harvard or McGill!"

This was always stated quite emphatically, as if it was a fact, that there were no other choices. At the time, this didn't mean that much to me, but I stored the information away for future reference. Then one day in Miss Hickson's Grade 5 class we were asked to name the university that we would like to go to. I immediately blurted out "Harvard or McGill" believing I had pretty well covered all of the options. Boy, was I surprised when some of the other kids yelled out a series of strange names like U. of T., UCLA, Cambridge, McMaster, UBC, Queen's, Cornell, Western, and others.

Miss Hickson went on to explain that there were many universities and colleges (in fact hundreds) across North America. This was definitely news to me at the time. She then stated that Montreal's McGill University was considered by most people to be among the very best in Canada. Of course that confirmed everything that I had heard over the dinner table in London. So from then on, for me, McGill was the place to be if you were going to go to university in Canada.

After that, I became very McGill-conscious. My ears would perk up whenever I heard the name mentioned on the tv or radio. I would notice McGill references and articles in newspapers and magazines. McGill jackets would stand out in a crowd for me. At one point I even bought McGill track pants to wear to high school.

When I was 13 years old my dad moved to Montreal. This was a big deal for me at the time, because not only did it mean Montreal, an exciting new city to visit, but it also meant I would be close to McGill University. I would travel there by bus every second weekend to stay with my dad. On those weekends, my heart would always beat a little faster when we would go by the old greystone buildings of the McGill campus, nestled half way up beautiful Mount Royal in the heart of the city.

When I was 15 I traveled to Montreal with the Ottawa Lion's Club track team. The meet was held at McGill's indoor track and field center. I felt at home immediately. In fact, for me it somehow felt like coming home. The corridor walls were plastered with photos of McGill sports heroes of the past. For some reason I don't fully understand, I felt proud of these bygone stars, and somehow strangely connected to them.

As I got older, I came to appreciate McGill's reputation as an international center for higher learning. Many famous and accomplished people have taught there and/or graduated from there. World famous pioneers like Linus Pauling and Norman Bethune. There were personal and family connections to McGill as well. Stephen Leacock had taught there for many years while spending his summers in my dad's birthplace, Orillia, Ontario. My dad's favorite poet, Leonard Cohen had graduated from McGill.

During my last two years at high school I worked harder than ever, intent on keeping my average in the mid-80s to make sure that I would have a chance to get in to McGill when the time came. I really focused on my English literature and world issues courses since I was interested in applying for political science or sociology, eventually doing an honors degree in International Development.

As I came to know Montreal, I realized how McGill and Montreal fit so perfectly together - a world-class international city, hosting a world-class international university. As one walks up McGill-College Avenue approaching the McGill campus, one sees the university and its mountain reflected in the windows of the high-rise office towers, opposite. Each one, a perfect reflection of the other.

Now, as I contemplate the possibility of attending McGill as a student, a lump forms in my throat as I realize how close I am to achieving that childhood dream. If I am accepted, it will be my turn to contribute to the continued building of that institution's international reputation for excellence. It's an awesome challenge that I definitely want to be a part of.

Admission Essay: Sample 4 (career and personal goals)

What are your career goals and why have you chosen that particular path. Where do you see yourself in ten years?

One of my best friends from when we were toddlers knew from the time she was eight or nine years-old that she wanted to be a doctor - no ifs, ands, or buts. Susan was going to be a doctor and that was it. The funny thing is, just last week Susan was accepted into her second medical school. I'm sure that she will do well in her studies and will become a great doctor.

It hasn't been quite so straightforward for me. In fact, to be perfectly honest I don't yet have any fixed career goals. But I do know some general directions that I want to go in, both professionally and personally. I just don't yet have a fix on a specific job or career path that I want to pursue.

My experiences both in and around high school have shown me some things I am good at and some things that I like to do more than others. For example, I love working face-to-face and shoulder-to-shoulder with other people, especially if we are working towards a common goal. I realized this when I worked as a co-organizer on a campaign to raise funds for cancer research. I adored the feeling of working with others for a great cause. I liked the concept of being able to help other people suffering or in need.

My work as a volunteer with handicapped and learning disabled children was also very rewarding for me. I enjoyed being around these kids and experiencing their innocence and their unconditional love whenever I would do the smallest thing to help them. These kids are not always easy to work with but the rewards can be great. It was nice to be able to make a small difference in someone's life every day, even if it might seem to be relatively minor stuff to some, in the big scheme of things.

I love writing, especially about current issues. Working as a feature writer on the school paper for the last two years of high school was like a dream come true for me. Since I had the "world issues beat" I was given carte blanche to focus on whatever I considered the more important issues on this planet right now. Pressing issues, like infant mortality, child poverty, and the general exploitation of children, especially in developing countries. I really enjoyed researching these subjects and writing articles about them. Again, by exposing these issues to a larger audience I felt I was helping people in suffering or need, at least indirectly.

This would explain why I have applied for admission into a general arts program with political science or sociology as my majors. I believe that during my studies in these areas I will develop a much clearer idea about which specific career path I might want to follow. In the meantime, I will continue to learn more about who I am and what this world is all about.

As for where I see myself ten years from now? Who can really know? There's no point in pretending that I know where I'll be or what I'll be doing. What I do wish though, is that ten years from now I will be happy and successful in whatever profession I will have evolved into during my university career. More than anything, I hope that at that time I will still be working, learning, and creating - and changing too!

I don't ever want to get "stuck" in one place in my development, either as a professional or a person. Ten years from now, if I can honestly say that I don't know what I'll be doing ten years from then, I'll know I'm on the right path. After all, I believe we're all here to keep on learning - forever.

Admission Essay: Sample 5 (social issues and concerns)

Discuss some of the main issues that concern you at the local, national, or international level.

"You're seeing the glass as half-empty again" my dad would invariably say to me as soon as I would launch into one of my frequent tirades about some new social injustice I had just discovered in my high school World Issues class. "Don't forget to look at the other side of the equation" he would admonish me.

Even now as I look back at one of those discussions that occurred just six months ago, I realize how my thinking has changed. I think I'm starting to see the big picture more than I used to. I'm starting to realize that many issues are very easy to react to at the basic gut level, but when one looks at them more carefully the picture is frequently much more complex and the "right" answer is not always so cut-and-dried anymore.

Mind you, this doesn't apply to everything. Some things are just plain wrong. War for example. Both sides may have a legitimate case but murdering each other's citizens can never be justified. Sexual abuse of children is another. This is sick and inexcusable under any circumstances. Essentially, I believe that all forms of violence against the human race are fundamentally wrong.

While working on a couple of projects in my final year of high school I had a chance to do some literature research into a number of these issues. What I found was very interesting. I came to realize that there are many social issues and conditions that aren't quite as straightforward as the ones I mentioned above.

For example, most people are not aware that by far the largest killer of human beings on this planet is indoor air pollution, estimated to kill 2.8 million people every year, mostly in the developing world. That's right, I said million. Yet, when we read our newspapers and listen to our politicians we never hear about this problem. Instead they go on-and-on about things like mad cow disease and the West Nile virus. Yes, it is unfortunate that some people are dying of these. However, the fact is that these two conditions together have killed fewer than one thousand people worldwide, ever. Compare this with 2.8 million human beings killed annually by indoor air pollution that is directly related to ignorance and living in poverty.

Global warming is another issue that I think is very important but one that is also being distorted and blown way out of proportion by the media and special interest groups. The fact is, that even the scientists can't agree on exactly what is going to happen in the future, and their estimates are wildly different. So, I can understand the reluctance of the U.S. government and some others to resist immediate implementation of the Kyoto protocol. Instead, they believe in a phased adoption of the Kyoto measures because immediate implementation would cost billions of dollars and throw the economies of the major developed countries into chaos. This would benefit no one, and would cause more pain and suffering than the short-term effects of global warming.

There are a number of other global issues that also interest me, including: human poverty and starvation, environmental issues in general, and biodiversity.

An aspect of all of this that really interests me goes back to my dad's analogy about the glass. Is it half-full or half-empty? Why do the media, politicians, and special interest groups tend to jump on the bandwagon of negativity on just about every major social issue? Is this healthy? Maybe if we're always preparing for the worst case scenario all the time, we can't go wrong. But then, what about our tendency to focus on the wrong things due to all of the hype surrounding the "designer" issues of the day?

These kinds of questions fascinate me. I guess that explains why I was drawn to apply for admission into a political science program majoring in world issues. After that, I think would like to enroll in a masters program in journalism in which I could focus on covering issues related to the developing world and the future of the human race. I would like to be able to add some balance to that coverage.

COMMERCIAL WRITING SERVICES – COLLEGE ADMISSION ESSAYS

There are numerous Web sites offering various levels and types of service to assist people in the writing of essay admissions of every description. Some of these sites also offer other writing services for related documents such as recommendation letters and college application letters.

The following chapter on "Online Resource Links" includes a section titled "College Admission Essay Links." That section contains more than 20 researched links to Web sites offering paid writing services and/or free information on writing college admission essays.

Hiring one of these services to edit and/or write an essay for you can be a fairly costly proposition. So, I have decided to do some additional research to help you select the service best for you, should you decide to hire one.

Accordingly, at the time of writing this I am planning to do some additional research into a number of these writing services and to produce a short "Buyers Guide." This guide will reduce the time it will take you to research these services and will help you select the best service for you.

I expect to offer this Buyers Guide as a Free Bonus download for all purchasers of *Instant Recommendation Letter Kit.*

ONLINE RESOURCE LINKS

There are literally thousands of Web sites and pages that contain information related to the writing of letters of recommendation and college admission essays.

For example, the week I compiled the following list I did some testing on www.google.com. When I entered the phrase "recommendation letter" google came back with 1,140,000 links! For the phrase "college admission essay", 145,000 relevant links were found.

So, in order to find the most relevant and useful links, I carefully checked out the top 100 links that google.com returned for each of the above phrases.

Accordingly, the following is a researched "short-list" of more than 80 links that I have compiled as the most useful and relevant links on the Web related to "recommendation letters" and "college admission essays".

How-To Information Links

Sample Recommendation letter... A letter of recommendation can be tricky
http://www.writinghelp-central.com/recommendation-letter.html

EastChance.com - How to write a Recommendation letter
http://www.eastchance.com/howto/rec_let.asp

Recommendation letter- Create reference letters
http://www.boxfreeconcepts.com/reco/index.html

Article - Recommendation Letters Demystified
http://www.writinghelp-central.com/article-recommendation-letter.html

How To Write A Letter Of Recommendation When Students Apply To Undergraduate Or Graduate Programs In America
http://ieie.nsc.ru:8101/~eac/fair_97/letter_recommend.htm

Writing a Letter of Recommendation
http://www.clarkpersonnel.com/html/resources_refletter.htm

Recommendation Letter Tips
http://www.staffsolutions.com/careerrecommendation.htm

Recommendation letter guidelines
http://www.sociology.camden.rutgers.edu/rec-ltr.htm

Nothing is more irritating to the referee than to be asked to write a letter of recommendation under pressure. ...
http://www.psych.hanover.edu/handbook/rec_letters2.html

How to Get Good Letters of Recommendation
http://www.psywww.com/careers/lettrec.htm

Writing Your First Letter of Recommendation
http://bokcenter.fas.harvard.edu/docs/TFTrecs.html

Advice on Letters of Recommendation
http://www.socialpsychology.org/rectips.htm

HSU Career Center: Letter of Recommendation
http://www.humboldt.edu/~career/services/tips/rec_tips.shtml

Letters of Recommendation and Reference
http://jobsearchtech.about.com/library/weekly/aa021400.htm

Refusal of Request for Letter of Recommendation
http://www.4hb.com/letters/ltrrefusref.html

The Medical School Letter of Recommendation
http://www.accepted.com/medical/letter_rec.htm

Department of Psychology's letter of recommendation service. ...
http://www.psych.ucsb.edu/ugrprg/ltrrec/rules.htm

EMPLOYMENT-RELATED SITES

Staff Recommendation Letter
http://www.iit.edu/~osa/applications/staff.html

Recommendation Letter from President & CEO of Applied Internet ...
http://www.cs.rit.edu/~gxf7855/recommendation_letter.htm

Award Recommendation Letter Writing
http://www.therotunda.net/sca/recommend-award.html

Recommendation Letter - Robert J. Cameron
http://fac.aii.edu/~rc0918/cred/rec.htm

Recommendation Letter
I am writing a letter of recommendation on behalf of Mark…
http://www.concertart.com/mark/letter3.html

The Graduate School Letter of Recommendation
http://www.accepted.com/grad/letter_rec.htm

Stellar Letters of Recommendation
http://teacher.scholastic.com/professional/futureteachers/recommendation.htm

CareerCity: Remember to send a thank-you note to anyone who writes a letter of recommendation for you.
http://www.careercity.com/content/interview/prep/letters.asp

Career Center letter writers may also write their recommendations for you…
http://career.berkeley.edu/Letter/Letter.stm

COLLEGE-RELATED SITES – TIPS AND SAMPLES

Letter of Recommendation Guidelines
http://www.upenn.edu/resliv/chas/join/ra/ref_guideline.html

Recommendation Letter Tips
http://www.infozee.com/indiatimes/application-issues/reco.htm

Caltech Graduate School Recommendation Letter Requests
http://www.design.caltech.edu/recomend.html

OSA Procedure for Requesting Recommendation
http://www.uic.edu/depts/mcam/osa/policy/letters.htm

Graduate School Request For Recommendation
http://www.colorado.edu/GraduateSchool/app/request.html

Recommendation Letter Guidelines, UGA Psychology Department
http://www.uga.edu/psychology/undergraduate/recletter.html

Recommendation Letter Martin Luther King, Jr., Memorial Committee.
http://www.bc.edu/bc_org/svp/mlkmc/academic.html

Recommendation Letter Advice for Applicants Applying To Graduate Schools Of The Health Professions
http://www.sunysb.edu/healthed/Text/letters.html

Recommendation letter guidelines
http://www.sociology.camden.rutgers.edu/rec-ltr.htm

The Letter of Recommendation Chaminade College Preparatory School
http://members.telocity.com/~jp4121/recommendation.html

Sample Letter of Recommendation
http://www.lehigh.edu/~village/Apply/sampleletter.html

Sample Letter of Recommendation for Rodica Simion
http://www.math.rutgers.edu/~zeilberg/simion/recom.html

Winning Scholarships: Writing letters of recommendation…
http://www.utpress.utoronto.ca/howell/chap08.html

Sample Request for Letter of Recommendation
http://www.med.stanford.edu/school/smysp/nojava/prepare/sampreq.html

COLLEGE-RELATED SITES - RECOMMENDATION LETTER FORMS

Recommendation Letter FormUniversity of Washington Physics Research ...
http://int.phys.washington.edu/REU/2002/reu4.html

UMass Lowell. Recommendation Letter
http://129.63.50.205/Online_Application/reco_us.html

Recommendation Letter Princeton in Beijing June 21 - August 17, 2002
http://www.princeton.edu/pib/recommendation.pdf

Letter of Recommendation Department of Information Science and Telecommunications
http://www.sis.pitt.edu/~dist/applications/recomm.html

Graduate School Of The University Of Florida Letter Of Recommendation.
http://gradschool.rgp.ufl.edu/education/recommendation.html

Optional Practical Training Recommendation Letter
http://www.ia.uconn.edu/PDF/f1student_recletter.pdf

Arizona Graduate Program in Public Health: Recommendation Letter
http://www.ahsc.arizona.edu/pub-hlth/appltr.htm

Hayward. School Of Business/Graduate Letter Of Recommendation.
http://sbegrad.csuhayward.edu/html/recommendation_letter.html

Recommendation Letter: School Of Graduate Studies. Alcorn State U.
www.alcorn.edu/academic/academ/gmajor/recommend.htm

Letter of Recommendation and Release Form
http://www.uprs.edu/rec.html

Letter of Recommendation – Graduate School, University of Mississippi
http://www.olemiss.edu/depts/psychology/Recommendation.html

Letter of Recommendation - Dept. of Human Services, Graduate Studies
http://www.wright.edu/sogs/gradapp/lor.html

UCSB Letter of Recommendation Form(s)
http://www.graddiv.ucsb.edu/admissions/forms/rec.html

Confidential Letter of Recommendation
http://www.coe.neu.edu/COE/grad_school/recommend.html

NSF and UCSD Department of Physics Undergraduate Research Program
Letter of Recommendation
http://physics.ucsd.edu/students/reu/refer.html

Graduate Degree Letter of Recommendation: New Mexico State University
www.nmsu.edu/~english/programs/referral.html

Letter Of Recommendation - University Of Western Ontario Epidemiology
http://www.uwo.ca/epidem/lor.htm

RECOMMENDATION LETTER SERVICES

EssayEdge: Recommendation Letter Editing ($24.95+).
http://www.essayedge.com/college/editing/recletter.shtml

Monster: A Few Tips on How to Write a Letter of Recommendation.
http://content.monster.com/resume/resources/recommendation/

Letter-of-recommendation.com
Do you need someone to write a letter of recommendation?
http://www.letter-of-recommendation.com/

BestSchoolsUSA - The recommendation letter is just another tool
http://www.bestschoolsusa.com/references.html

College Admissions: Four Steps To Getting Perfect College Recommendations
http://www.freschinfo.com/admissions-4steps.phtml

ResumeEdge.com: Letter of Recommendation Help…
http://www.resumeedge.com/recentgrads/careercenter/recommendations

COLLEGE ADMISSION ESSAY LINKS

About College Admissions…editing services range from basic editing to helping brainstorm and then develop ideas.
http://www.aboutcollegeadmissions.com

Accepted.com - The Graduate School Letter of Recommendation
http://www.accepted.com/grad/letter_rec.htm

Admission Essays... College Admission Essay Writing Resources…
http://www.admissionsessays.com/

ArtSchools.com - 100 Successful College Application Essays…
http://www.artschools.com/applying

The Best College Admission Essays by Mark A. Stewart, Cynthia Muchnick
http://www.databank.oxydex.com/exam_prep_information/College_Admission.html

College Admission Essay. The Cambridge Essay Service.
http://world.std.com/~edit/tips6.htm

The college admission essay is an important part of your application. These links will show you how to create the best essay...
http://www.collegeapps.about.com/cs/admissionessay

College admission essays and personal statement assistance…
http://www.collegeadmissionsessays.com

College admission essay writing. Check this out to get some great help…
http://examplesessaysfree.com/admission

College Admission Essays: Mirrors, Not Calculators By Addie L. Gayoso, Saint Mary's College Admission Counselor ...
http://www.saintmarys.edu/~admoff/AdmissionQuarterly/QrtlyStu.html

College-Essays.com. Premium editing for serious applicants…
http://www.college-essays.com/pricing.htm

College Super Mall - College essay critique and evaluation of your application essay and student personal statement. http://www.collegesupermall.com

College admission essay services. Professional help to make sure that your college application stands out from the crowd. ...
http://www.editmenow.com

EssayEdge.com. College admission essay editing and writing service...
http://www.essayedge.com/

Great-Term-Papers: college admission, entrance, and application essays ...
http://www.great-term-paper-sites.com/term-paper/most-popular.html

Suggestions for Writing a Winning College Admission Essay...
http://www.sru.edu/depts/admissio/lagnese/essays.htm

Writing the college admission essay
http://www.oldicpac.indiana.edu/infoseries

Writing the College Admission Essay by Nancy Davis Griffin Director of Admission Saint Joseph's College of Maine.
http://www.reslife.net/html/preparing_1200a.html

IEFA.org Admission Information and Links. College Admission Essay & Resume Editing Services!
http://www.iefa.org/links/admissioninfo.html

MyEssay.com. College Admission Essay Resources and Help...
http://www.home.okstate.edu/homepages.nsf/toc/ed-essay

PointsIn Case.com college admission essay service...
http://www.pointsincase.com/essay.htm

Southwestern University - Writing the college admission essay is crucial.
http://www.southwestern.edu/admission-finaid/tips.html

NOTES

BUYERS GUIDE

Online Writing Services for...
- College Admission Essays
- Recommendation Letters

by Shaun Fawcett, M.B.A.

A Bonus Supplement To...

"Instant Recommendation Letter Kit"

RECOMMENDATION LETTERS: employment, college...
REFERENCE LETTERS: employment, character, general...
COMMENDATION LETTERS: employment, community service...
PERFORMANCE EVALUATION LETTERS: college, university...
COLLEGE ADMISSION ESSAYS...

http://www.instantrecommendationletterkit.com

eBook Solutions.net
Saving You Time and Money

A SUPPLEMENTARY ANNEX TO – "INSTANT RECOMMENDATION LETTER KIT"

Copyright © 2002 by Shaun R. Fawcett

All rights reserved. No part of this book may be reproduced or transmitted in any form, by any means, without written permission from the author, except a reviewer, who may quote brief passages for a review.

National Library of Canada Cataloguing in Publication Data

Fawcett, Shaun, 1949-
Instant recommendation letter kit [electronic resource] : how to write winning letters of recommendation

Includes bibliographical references.

ISBN 0-9684297-5-0

1. Employment references. 2. Letter writing. I. Title.
HF5549.5.R45F38 2002   808'.06665   C2002-902875-2

Final Draft Publications
1501 Notre-Dame West, Suite No. 5
Montreal QC, Canada H3C 1L2

http://www.writinghelp-central.com

Disclaimer

This book was written as a guide only, and does not claim to be the final definitive word on any of the subjects covered. The statements made and opinions expressed are the personal observations and assessments of the author based on his own experiences and were not intended to prejudice any party. There may be errors or omissions in this guide. As such, the author or publisher does not accept any liability or responsibility for any loss or damage that may have been caused, or alleged to have been caused, through use of the information contained in this manual. Errors or omissions will be corrected in future editions, provided the publisher receives written notification of such.

TABLE OF CONTENTS

INTRODUCTION 1
   ADMISSION ESSAY SITES 1
   RECOMMENDATION LETTER SITES 2
   NOTES ON METHODOLOGY 2

ADMISSION ESSAY SITE REVIEWS 4
   REVIEW CRITERIA DEFINITIONS 4
   DETAILED SERVICE REVIEWS 5
      AboutCollegeAdmissions.com 6
      Accepted.com 9
      AdmissionsConsultants.com 12
      AdmissionEssays.com 15
      College-Essays.com 18
      CollegeSuperMall.com 21
      EditMeNow.com 24
      EssayEdge.com 27
      IvyEdge.com 31

COMPARISON OF ADMISSION ESSAY SERVICES 35
   COST COMPARISON TABLE 35
   ASSUMPTIONS 36
   HOW TO CHOOSE 37

RECOMMENDATION LETTER SERVICES 39
   EMPLOYMENT-RELATED 39
   COLLEGE-RELATED 40
   GENERAL LETTER-WRITING SERVICES 40

COMPARISON OF RECOMMENDATION LETTER SERVICES 41
   COST COMPARISON TABLE 41
   ASSUMPTIONS 42
   HOW TO CHOOSE 42

INTRODUCTION

While researching and writing my recent eBook *Instant Recommendation Letter Kit* I realized that it's a "jungle" out there when it comes to looking for professional help for writing letters of recommendation and/or college admission essays. In fact, it's confusing trying to sort out and compare the many Web-based businesses offering various types and levels of writing services on a fee basis.

As I checked some of these online Services out, I also realized just how difficult and time-consuming it is to navigate through the many sites offering these services and to sort out comparable information in order to make an informed decision as to which service to choose. (In fact, it took me more than 40 hours to conduct the online research when preparing this guide).

Accordingly, the primary purpose of this guide is to save you, the reader, a good deal of time, trouble, and money in trying to find your way through the information maze and figure out which service is best for you.

ADMISSION ESSAY SITES

As I said, it took many hours of research to narrow the list down to what I consider to be the top few Web sites offering these types of services for the writing of college admission essays.

These types of Services were particularly tricky to research. There are literally scores of Web sites claiming to offer admission essay services. Because of the various service possibilities (i.e. undergraduate, graduate, MBA, etc.) some of these sites are complex with literally hundreds of pages of content and links.

However, let me insert a note of caution here. Once you roll your sleeves up and take a careful look at these sites, many are not legitimate service sites.

In fact, many are affiliate sites offering free content, solely to attract visitors to their Web site. But when it comes to the actual writing services, these sites simply provide affiliate links to one of the primary online Services. (In other words, they receive a commission if you go to one of the primary admission sites using their link and then make a purchase).

Accordingly, affiliate sites are not covered in this guide. Only direct providers of admission essay services are included in this assessment.

RECOMMENDATION LETTER SITES

In researching writing services sites that offer recommendation letter writing, I was surprised at how few of them there really are. It turns out that, on the subject of "recommendation letters", there is lots of free advice out there on how to write your own, but not that many professional services that will do it for you.

Of course there is a natural crossover between recommendation letter sites and admission essay sites, since recommendation letters are often required as part of the college program application process. However, there are also resume and letter writing sites that offer recommendation letter writing for the other types of recommendation letters that are not related to college applications.

The different types of letters of recommendation are discussed in detail in *Instant Recommendation Letter Kit.*

I have made every effort to ensure that the Web sites I have listed here are legitimate providers of professional recommendation letter writing services.

NOTES ON METHODOLOGY

As already stated, the primary purpose of this report is to give the reader a quick review and easy comparison reference guide on the extent of coverage and the cost of the various Services available.

The following pages contain a summary of the services available at each of the above-listed sites. My main focus in this analysis has been the specific services offered and the prices charged for those services.

The information that I have provided is derived from each Web site. In a few cases, I also e-mailed the Service for clarification of their offer. When applicable, that information is also included in the following profiles.

Since I haven't personally used any of these Service companies, my assessment is based strictly on my personal and professional evaluation of what is offered on each Web site, and how it compares with the other sites being reviewed.

Accordingly, the service profiles that follow are presented in alphabetical order. I have not attempted to rank them since, as already stated, I have not personally used any of these Services.

Please note that I have not used any affiliate links in this report, so I have no vested interest in you using any particular Service.

This information has been compiled for the convenience of the reader. Use the information to assist you in choosing the Service that best suits your overall needs.

Errors or Omissions

As stated in the "Disclaimer" statement on the title page of this report, any errors or omissions will be corrected in future editions, provided that the publisher receives written notification of such. So, if you notice an error or omission while working with this guide, please send me an e-mail at the address link below, and I will make every effort to ensure that the appropriate revisions are made before the next Buyers Guide is released.
info@instantrecommendationletterkit.com

ADMISSION ESSAY SITE REVIEWS

Although the design and contents of the sites reviewed vary widely, in order to make comparisons possible, it is necessary to present the results in a standardized fashion.

Accordingly, the information gathered during my review of each Web site is broken down under six (6) main headings for comparison purposes. Following is a list of those headings with a brief explanation of what each one covers.

REVIEW CRITERIA DEFINITIONS

Service Statement:

This is the primary overall statement of purpose or mission taken directly from the opening page of the Web site. Basically it's their "what we do" statement. In most cases I have presented this text verbatim as presented on the Web site.

Claim To Fame:

This is the "why use us" statement usually found on the opening page of the Web site. It's their "unique selling proposition" or USP. This statement is supposed to explain what makes this Service unique, and why you should choose it over the competition. In a few cases, I deleted redundant statements or joined a number of phrases from various places on the page. However, I never added my own words to theirs.

NOTE: *I have used italics in the two sections defined above throughout the document to indicate that the text is drawn directly or quoted from the Service's Web site.*

Subjects Covered:

This section provides a breakdown of the specific services that the Web site says they provide. I have broken it down into two categories: *Admissions Services* and *Other Related Services*.

Admissions Services are those related directly to the physical preparation of an admission essay and support documents.

Other Related Services are free support services offered on the Web site or other fee-based services not directly related to the admissions process. Resume writing and general recommendation letters are two examples of this.

Fees and Charges:

These are the fees and charges published on the Web site of the service at the time when this survey was done. In most cases, the tables that present the fees and charges for each Service in one place are in my own format. I often had to scour the Web sites to find all of the charges for the various services provided. Also, each Service uses a different presentation format.

General Comments:

This is my overall assessment of the Service and Web site reviewed. In addition, in some cases I have made note of anything unique or unusual that I noticed while evaluating the Service.

Bottom Line:

This statement relates to the cost of the service. I felt it would be helpful for comparison purposes to provide a rough cost-comparison benchmark. The case I have used to estimate cost is: the preparation from scratch of a basic 1,000 word basic college admission essay.

Based on my personal experience writing such essays, the professional time required to write and revise such an essay to the finished, final product stage would be about 3.5 to 5 hours in total.

Because these writing Services work from their own templates and do this all of the time, I estimate that it would take them four (4) hours, at most. This would include drafting an essay or personal statement from scratch based on point form information provided by the client, and then performing up to two (2) light edits based on client feedback, to arrive at a final product.

DETAILED SERVICE REVIEWS

Subject to the above, the following pages contain my detailed write-ups for each of the Admission Essay Services reviewed in this document.

(Please note that at the time this list was compiled all of these links were tested and found to be in working order).

AboutCollegeAdmissions.com

http://www.aboutcollegeadmissions.com

Service Statement:

(Taken from the Web site of the online Service being reviewed).

Whether you are applying to private or public college, Ivy League schools, liberal arts schools, professional schools, or state schools, we offer you a full range of resources. Feel free to use the many resources on this site--free Sample Essays, our excellent free Essay Writing Course, free Interviewing Tips, free tips on how to choose your college, and free profiles of success--which provide you with information to help strengthen your overall application.

Claim to Fame:

(Taken from the Web site of the online Service being reviewed).

Our team includes former Harvard admission workers, former Harvard faculty, former Harvard and Stanford advisors, Oxford PhD-holders, Harvard Business School and Harvard Law School graduates, Fulbright Scholars, and professionals with undergraduate degrees from Harvard, Yale and Stanford.

Our mentoring and advice have helped students get into college, business school, law school, education school, and PhD programs at institutions such as Harvard, Stanford, Yale, UC Berkeley, the University of Chicago, the University of Virginia, Georgetown, New York University, UC Santa Cruz, MIT, and Oxford University (among many others!). Likewise, our editing and mentoring has helped students win Fulbright Scholarships, Rotary Awards, Most Valuable Student awards, and all-expense-paid foreign traveling scholarships.

Subjects Covered:

(These are subject areas specifically covered by the service as per their Web site).

Admission Services:
("Yes" in the "Covered?" column indicates specific mention on their Web site).

COVERED?	SUBJECT AREA	SPECIFIC PRODUCTS/SERVICES
Yes	College (undergraduate)	Admission Essays
Yes	Graduate School	Admission Essays
Yes	Business School/MBA	Application Essays
Yes	Law School	Admission Essays
Yes	Medical School	Admission Essays

Other Related Services:

("Yes" in the "Covered?" column indicates specific mention on their Web site).

COVERED?	PRODUCT OR SERVICE	SPECIFIC PRODUCT/SERVICE
Yes	Advisory Service	Essay Evaluation
	Recommendation Letters	
	Resumes	
Yes	Free Samples	All Types
Yes	Free Tips	FAQs, College Interview Tips.
	Free Newsletter	
Yes?	Free Course	Essay Writing Course
	Bookstore	

Fees and Charges:

(As published on their Web site July 1, 2002).

Essay Editing Fees:

LENGTH OF ESSAY (WORDS)	BASIC EDITING ($)	BASIC EDITING SECOND REVIEW SERVICE ($)	ESSAY DEVELOPMENT ($)	OPINION AND PROOFREADING SERVICE ($)
900 words or less	57.95	30.95	129.95	35.95
901-1200 words	82.95	35.95	159.95	45.95
Over 1200 words	82.95 plus $20 for each additional 1-200 words	35.95 plus $10 for each additional 1-200 words	159.95 plus $30 for each additional 1-200 words	45.95 plus $10 for each additional 1-200 words

| Short essays (less than 250 words) | 36.95 | 17.95 | 57.95 | 25.95 |

MBA Essay Editing Fees:

SERVICE APPLICATION	BASIC EDITING ($)	ESSAY DEVELOPMENT ($)
First set of MBA application essays	$165 (includes all required essays for 1 entire MBA application)	$230 (includes all required essays for 1 entire MBA application)
Second set of MBA application essays	$150 (includes all required essays for 1 entire MBA application)	$200 (includes all required essays for 1 entire MBA application)
Each additional set of MBA application essays	$135 (includes all required essays for 1 entire MBA application)	$175 (includes all required essays for 1 entire MBA application)

General Comments:

Although the Web site mentions that they do all types of admission essays, this Service appears to specialize in essays for basic college admission at the undergraduate level, as well as in MBA application essays. They also mention a free Essay Writing Course in their write-up, but I couldn't find it.

Bottom Line:

Based on the information presented on the Web site, my best estimate of the minimum it would cost to develop a 1,000 word basic college admission essay from scratch using this Service is about $160.

For a cost comparison with the other Services, see the Cost Comparison Table in the final chapter.

Accepted.com

http://www.accepted.com

Service Statement:

(Taken from the Web site of the online Service being reviewed).

Accepted.com is the premier admissions consulting and application essay editing service. Our purpose? Helping you gain acceptance to a top school and land a great job. How? With exceptional advising and editing services along with a treasure-trove of information on: Business School Admissions, Medical School Admissions, Law School Admissions, Grad School Admissions, College Admissions, and Resumes.

Claim to Fame:

(Taken from the Web site of the online Service being reviewed).

Accepted.com gives you the edge you need in these competitive times. The Wall Street Journal praised us for helping applicants overcome the "most daunting part" of the admissions process -- the essays. Explore our catalog of services to discover the many ways Accepted.com can strengthen your application to Top Choice U. And after completing your education, Accepted.com can help again. Our resume section overflows with insightful job-search strategies, and our professional resume writers can help you land that plum job.

Subjects Covered:

(These are subject areas specifically covered by the service as per their Web site).

Admission Services:

("Yes" in the "Covered?" column indicates specific mention on their Web site).

COVERED?	SUBJECT AREA	SPECIFIC PRODUCTS/SERVICES
Yes	College (undergraduate)	Admission Essays
		Wait-List Letters
Yes	Graduate School	Admission Essays
		Recommendation Letters
		Wait-List Letters
		Admissions Consulting

Yes	Business School/MBA	Application Essays
		Recommendation Letters
		Wait-List Letters
		Application Review
		Admissions Consulting
Yes	Law School	Admission Essays
		Recommendation Letters
		Wait-List Letters
		Application Review
		Admissions Consulting
Yes	Medical School	Admission Essays
		Application Essays
		Recommendation Letters
		Wait-List Letters
		Application Review
		Admissions Consulting

Other Related Services:

("Yes" in the "Covered?" column indicates specific mention on their Web site).

COVERED?	PRODUCT OR SERVICE	SPECIFIC PRODUCT/SERVICE
Yes	Advisory Service	Essay Evaluation
Yes	Resumes	Resumes and CVs
		Resume Cover Letters
Yes	Free Samples	Essays and Letters
Yes	Free Tips	Interview Tips.
Yes	Free Newsletter	Monthly
	Free Course	
Yes	Bookstore	Admission Related Books

Fees and Charges:

(As published on their Web site July 1, 2002).

SERVICES PROVIDED	REG. RATE ($)	RUSH RATE ($)
Essay Writing (Admissions)		
Initial Essay	575 – 700	747 – 910

Subsequent Essays	425	553
Special Essay Package – Buy 7, Get 1 Free	3,125	3,400
Review/Edit/Consult (hourly rate)	150	195
Letter Writing (admissions)		
Letter of Recommendation	275 – 425	357 – 553
Wait-List Letter	300 – 425	390 – 553
Review/Edit (hourly rate)	150	195
Resume Writing		
Write a Resume or CV	350	455
Resume Cover Letter	125 – 175	162 – 228
Resignation Letter	75	98
Review/Edit (hourly rate)	150	195
Consulting, Editing, Reviewing		
Standard Hourly Rate	150	195

General Comments:

This is clearly a high-end premium service. I have to assume that the quality of the final product will be a reflection of the higher rates. Based on their published rates, you won't get away from here for much less than $600 for a basic college admission essay.

The extensive Web site has lots of useful resources that will help you in your preparation of draft material. It is one of the few Services that offers a free regular newsletter.

Bottom Line:

Based on the information presented on the Web site, my best estimate of the minimum it would cost to develop a 1,000 word basic college admission essay from scratch using this Service is about $575.

For a cost comparison with the other Services, see the Cost Comparison Table in the final chapter.

AdmissionsConsultants.com

http://www.admissionsconsultants.com/

Service Statement:

(Taken from the Web site of the online Service being reviewed).

AdmissionsConsultants^{SM} is a full-service, comprehensive admissions consulting firm. All of our admissions consultants are very highly qualified. Accordingly, we offer far more than simply essay editing to our clients as we understand that every selective college and business school, not to mention every medical school, routinely rejects applicants with grammatically correct essays and personal statements.

We are qualified to help you select the programs to which you wish to attend, assess your admissions probabilities at those institutions, help you craft the personalized admissions strategy best suited to your chosen schools and unique background, and then help you execute the strategy through the entire application. This includes: essays, personal statements, letters of recommendation extracurricular activities, and admissions interviews.

Claim to Fame:

(Taken from the Web site of the online Service being reviewed).

Before AdmissionsConsultants^{SM} was formed, the company's founder and president, David Petersam, successfully guided several friends and acquaintances through the turbulent admissions process that encircles the nation's elite schools. After witnessing how successfully his admissions strategies were transferred to these individuals and being told by these same applicants that he should start an admissions consulting firm, AdmissionsConsultants was formed.

AdmissionsConsultants has helped clients gain admission into many different universities and this list, which is quite extensive, includes such top schools as Harvard, Stanford, Yale, Northwestern, U. Penn, Oxford, Michigan, Virginia, MIT, and London Business School. The chances are quite high that we have helped a client gain admission into your top-choice schools.

Subjects Covered:

(These are subject areas specifically covered by the service as per their Web site).

Admission Services:

("Yes" in the "Covered?" column indicates specific mention on their Web site).

COVERED?	SUBJECT AREA	SPECIFIC PRODUCTS/SERVICES
Yes	**College (undergraduate)**	**Admission Essays** **Personal Statements** **Letters of Recommendation** **Admissions Consulting**
	Graduate School	
Yes	**Business School/MBA**	**Application Essays** **Personal Statements** **Letters of Recommendation** **Resume Editing** **Admissions Consulting**
	Law School	
Yes	**Medical School**	**Admission Essays** **Personal Statements** **Letters of Recommendation** **Admissions Consulting**

Other Related Services:

("Yes" in the "Covered?" column indicates specific mention on their Web site).

COVERED?	PRODUCT OR SERVICE	SPECIFIC PRODUCT/SERVICE
Yes	**Advisory Service**	**Essay Evaluation**
Yes	**Recommendation Letters**	**Advertsing and Writing**
Yes	**Resumes**	**Editing**
	Free Samples	
Yes	**Free Tips**	**FAQs, SAT and GMAT Advice**
	Free Newsletter	
	Free Course	
Yes	**Bookstore**	**Admission Related Books**

Fees and Charges:

(As published on their Web site July 1, 2002).

Services Provided	Hourly Rate ($)
College Admission Essays	95
MBA Application Essays	125
Medical School Admission Essays	130

General Comments:

This service appears to focus entirely on admission essays for college (undergraduate), business school/MBA, and medical school. Law and graduate admissions are not even mentioned. I have the impression that they may be a little thin on the medical school admission side of things since they devote much less space and information to that service, compared with the other two.

The details as to specifically what this service will do for you are somewhat sketchy and their fee schedule doesn't clarify things in this area.

Bottom Line:

Based on the information presented on the Web site, my best estimate of the minimum cost to develop a 1,000 word basic college admission essay from scratch using this Service is about $380.

For a cost comparison with the other Services, see the Cost Comparison Table in the final chapter.

AdmissionEssays.com

http://www.admissionsessays.com/

Service Statement:

(Taken from the Web site of the online Service being reviewed).

Admissions Essays is the premier personal statement development service on the Web. We provide all the necessary guidance to help our clients produce memorable, striking, and effective personal statements and admission essays to help them get into their schools of choice.

At AdmissionsEssays.Com we understand the competitive pressures you face in applying to college, professional, or graduate schools. AdmissionsEssays.Com is here to help. Our staff of professional writers are here to assist you in creating the most effective personal statements or admissions essays possible. Whether you already have an existing essay requiring critique, or you have not yet started on your essay, we provide services that are aimed at creating an engaging personal story from your own unique biographical facts.

Claim to Fame:

(Taken from the Web site of the online Service being reviewed).

AdmissionsEssays.Com writers and editors are graduates of top institutions, including the University of Pennsylvania and the University of California at Berkeley. Perhaps most importantly though, they love to write and create memorable, and striking essays. They possess the background and education necessary to create engaging and thoughtful sample essays that will help you in your quest to develop the best possible personal statement.

We are the most dedicated and professional service available today. Our teams of writers and staff have years of experience in this field and are here to help you create the most compelling admission essay possible. We offer all the tools you need in creating your own winning essay.

Subjects Covered:

(These are subject areas specifically covered by the service as per their Web site).

Admission Services:

("Yes" in the "Covered?" column indicates specific mention on their Web site).

COVERED?	SUBJECT AREA	SPECIFIC PRODUCTS/SERVICES
Yes	College (undergraduate)	Admission Essays Personal Statements
Yes	Graduate School	Admission Essays Personal Statements
Yes	Business School/MBA	Application Essays Personal Statements
Yes	Law School	Application Essays Personal Statements
Yes	Medical School	Admission Essays Personal Statements

Other Related Services:

("Yes" in the "Covered?" column indicates specific mention on their Web site).

COVERED?	PRODUCT OR SERVICE	SPECIFIC PRODUCT/SERVICE
	Advisory Service	
	Recommendation Letters	
	Resumes	
Yes	Free Samples	Essays, Personal Statements
Yes	Free Tips	Essay Writing Tips, Insider Tips
	Free Newsletter	
	Free Course	
	Bookstore	

Fees and Charges:

(As published on their Web site July 1, 2002).

SERVICES PROVIDED	REG. RATE ($)	RUSH RATE ($)
Essay Critique Services	165	225
Essay Development Services	285	385

General Comments:

A very good looking and well-designed Web site. So, at first glance this Service looks very impressive. However, after investigating further it becomes clear that this is essentially a basic essay writing and editing service run by a small group of key principals who have some background in admission essays writing.

The two primary services offered here are: essay critique service and essay development service. The critique service works from an essay already drafted by the client. The essay development service involves the development of a new essay from scratch based on information provided by the client.

Bottom Line:

Based on the information presented on the Web site, my best estimate of the minimum cost to develop a 1,000 word basic college admission essay from scratch using this Service is $285.

For a cost comparison with the other Services, see the Cost Comparison Table in the final chapter.

College-Essays.com

http://www.college-essays.com/index.htm

Service Statement:

(Taken from the Web site of the online Service being reviewed).

Our mission is to help you write the best possible application essay that honestly represents who you are, and what you are capable of. We help define you as a unique, capable and success-oriented individual.

Claim to Fame:

(Taken from the Web site of the online Service being reviewed).

Our team consists of professionals with advanced degrees from the nation's top universities, superior editing capabilities and a stellar track record. With every engagement, we renew our commitment to delivering outstanding results for you - our customer. The success and support of our clients has helped us become the premier essay editing service for serious applicants looking to be admitted to some of the world's most prestigious and competitive institutions.

We were founded in 1999. Our focus is our clients - helping them project their best attributes in the most persuasive manner possible. We do not rely on specializing in any set of schools, insider knowledge, or on formulae to second-guess an admission committee's hidden sweet spots. We do try to help bring a sense of clarity, purpose, thoughtfulness, and confidence to your essay writing. Our review staff is composed of senior management professionals, technical PhDs and MBAs from top US universities.

Our small size and editing team are our greatest strengths. We provide personalized attention to every client, and will remember you by name whenever you return - as many of our clients do. Our in-house editing staff has been the same since our inception, and we never outsource to part-time editors or students. The process of shaping an essay often requires discussion of personal and confidential issues. Our clients benefit from dealing with mature professionals and absolute respect for their privacy.

Subjects Covered:

(These are subject areas specifically covered by the service as per their Web site).

Admission Services:

("Yes" in the "Covered?" column indicates specific mention on their Web site).

Covered?	Subject Area	Specific Products/Services
Yes	College (undergraduate)	Admission Essays
Yes	Graduate School	Admission Essays
Yes	Business School/MBA	Application Essays
Yes	Law School	Application Essays
Yes	Medical School	Admission Essays
Yes	Engineering	Statements of Purpose

Other Related Services:

("Yes" in the "Covered?" column indicates specific mention on their Web site).

Covered?	Product or Service	Specific Product/Service
	Advisory Service	
	Recommendation Letters	
	Resumes	
Yes	Free Samples	Essays, Questions (small selection)
Yes	Free Tips	Essay Writing Tips (barebones)
	Free Newsletter	
	Free Course	
Yes	Bookstore	Some Links to amazon.com

Fees and Charges:

(As published on their Web site July 1, 2002).

Services Provided	Basic Essay 4 Days (600 words) ($)	Rush 2 Days (600 words) ($)	Super Rush 1 Day (600 words) ($)	Add. Cost Per Word (over 600) ($)
Quick Evaluation	49	79	--	0.10

Standard Editing	209	279	329	0.20
Platinum Editing	329	449	629	0.35
Essay Development (7-10 days)	549	--	--	0.45

General Comments:

Although these people claim to provide "premium editing for serious applicants" their Web site does not give me a very warm feeling inside. Relative to most of their competitors, they reveal very little of what they know and understand about writing these types of essays. I'm sure they must have qualified people who can draft a good essay, but based on the limited information on their Web site, hiring them would be a bit of an act of faith.

The Web site is sketchy at best as far as content is concerned, and very little tangible evidence is given that indicates that they are in fact, the best on the Net, as they claim to be.

Although they don't go into details on it, they are the only service reviewed that mentions "Engineering Statements of Purpose." Maybe they have some specialized expertise for these.

Bottom Line:

Based on the information presented on the Web site, my best estimate of what it the minimum cost to develop a 1,000 word basic college admission essay from scratch using this Service is $729. (They have a heavy per-word-charge over 600 words that drives the cost up quickly).

For a cost comparison with the other Services, see the Cost Comparison Table in the final chapter.

CollegeSuperMall.com

http://www.collegesupermall.com

Service Statement:

(Taken from the Web site of the online Service being reviewed).

CollegeSuperMall.com serves the needs of college and college-bound students, as well parents of high school students, & faculty across the USA. Our essay editing service is second to none! We take great pride in providing a qualityservice at reasonable prices. Over the years we've found that for many students, writing the essay is one of the most troublesome parts of the application process. It also appears to be one of the most misunderstood. Some students are fortunate enough to have English teachers who understand the nuances of an effective college application essay. These teachers are are able to guide them appropriately. However, not all students are this lucky, and that's why our essay evaluation services are so important!

Our mission, is to see that every student, whether right out of high school or whether a returning adult, uncover every option available to them. Our confidential report provides you the student, with a detailed report on all the financial aid awards for which you qualify. It also discloses vital information on your choices of colleges and majors, as well as a detailed examination of the job outlook and future career prospects based on your career selections.

Claim to Fame:

(Taken from the Web site of the online Service being reviewed).

Our dedicated staff is family-based, with assistance from outside experts ranging from CPAs to proof readers and editors. We proudly offer support and services in three distinct areas of the college selection process: College Planning, Financial Aid Planning, and Admission Essay Evaluation.

We recognize the college application process to be a stressful period for most families. It's a time when frustration and fear builds up and seems to take over. While some families are sadly misinformed, others suffer from information overflow. Our objective is to alleviate some of this pressure by offering a useful, customized, personal report that sorts everything out for you. Every report is prepared exclusively based on the specific student/family situation.

Subjects Covered:

(These are subject areas <u>specifically</u> covered by the service as per their Web site).

CollegeSuperMall.com provides essay editing and evaluation services only. It does not deveop essays from scratch.

Admission Services:

("Yes" in the "Covered?" column indicates <u>specific</u> mention on their Web site).

COVERED?	SUBJECT AREA	SPECIFIC PRODUCTS/SERVICES
Yes	College (undergraduate)	Admission Essays
	Graduate School	
	Business School/MBA	
	Law School	
	Medical School	
Yes	Sports Programs	Sports Resume

Other Related Services:

("Yes" in the "Covered?" column indicates <u>specific</u> mention on their Web site).

COVERED?	PRODUCT OR SERVICE	SPECIFIC PRODUCT/SERVICE
Yes	Advisory Service	Financial, Scholarships
	Recommendation Letters	
Yes	Resumes	Sports Resumes
	Free Samples	
Yes	Free Tips	Essays, Interviews, Scholarships
	Free Newsletter	
Yes	Free Course	Essay Writing Tutorial
	Bookstore	

Fees and Charges:

(As published on their Web site July 1, 2002)

SERVICES PROVIDED	0 – 500 WORDS ($)	501 – 1,000 WORDS ($)	1,001 – 1,500 WORDS ($)	1,501 – 2,000 WORDS ($)
Quick Appraisal	14.95	14.95	19.95	19.95

Full Evaluation	29.95	39.95	49.95	50.95
Expanded Service	119.95	119.95	179.95	179.95
Additional Resubmissions	15.00	15.00	20.00	20.00

General Comments:

This Web site and the service offering on it are somewhat confusing. You have to go to the "About Us" page to find out what they actually do. It would appear that this service deals with college (undergraduate) admission and application essays only. It evaluates and edits already-drafted essays and Does Not offer an essay development service.

The Web site gives the impression that they specialize in admission essays for sports programs. However, aside from some information on how to obtain sports scholarships, there is nothing to indicate that they have any special expertise in this area.

Bottom Line:

Based on the information presented on the Web site, my best estimate of the minimum cost to complete an *already-drafted* 1,000 word basic college admission essay using this service is $54.95.

For a cost comparison with the other Services, see the Cost Comparison Table in the final chapter.

EditMeNow.com

http://www.editmenow.com

Service Statement:

(Taken from the Web site of the online Service being reviewed).

EditMeNow.com specializes in working with high school students to turn admission essays into winning statements of purpose that will make college admission committees take notice. Our editing staff consists of National Merit Scholars and English graduate students—people who know what it takes to successfully get into college and write a strong essay.

Claim to Fame:

(Taken from the Web site of the online Service being reviewed).

EditMeNow.com was the first site to bring true editing and writing professionals to the Internet. Composed of a nationwide network of independently contracted professionals, EditMeNow helps you get it perfect the first time. None of our competitors can match our vast range of services or come close to our affordable prices. Why? Because most of our "competitors" are little more than a couple of guys working out of their dens. Our vast network of independent associates allows us to offer you greater resources at the most affordable prices on the Internet. Sample our services to learn why EditMeNow.com is the #1 document processing site on the Web.

The best part about our service is the affordability. Other web-based editing services charge upwards of $100 to edit a few thousand words! We offer the most thorough and comprehensive essay editing anywhere, and we do it for a fraction of the cost. After all, if you had that much money to throw around, you wouldn't need to be applying for scholarships, would you? Put our experience and expertise to work for you. Let EditMeNow.com make your essay strong enough to clear that final hurdle on your way to college success!

Subjects Covered:

(These are subject areas <u>specifically</u> covered by the service as per their Web site).

EditMeNow.com provides essay evaluation and editing services only. It does not deveop essays from scratch. (See note below re: Sample Essay Service).

Admission Services:

("Yes" in the "Covered?" column indicates <u>specific</u> mention on their Web site).

COVERED?	SUBJECT AREA	SPECIFIC PRODUCTS/SERVICES
Yes	College (undergraduate)	Admission Essays
	Graduate School	
	Business School/MBA	
	Law School	
	Medical School	
Yes	Scholarship	Application Essays

Other Related Services:

("Yes" in the "Covered?" column indicates <u>specific</u> mention on their Web site).

COVERED?	PRODUCT OR SERVICE	SPECIFIC PRODUCT/SERVICE
	Advisory Service	
	Recommendation Letters	
Yes	Resumes	By an affiliated Web service.
Yes	Samples – Not Free	Special Sample Essay for a fee.
	Free Tips	
	Free Newsletter	
	Free Course	
	Bookstore	

Fees and Charges:

(As published on their Web site July 1, 2002).

SERVICES PROVIDED	0 – 1,100 WORDS ($)	1,101 – 1,500 WORDS ($)	1,501 – 2,000 WORDS ($)	2,001 – 3,000 WORDS ($)	3,000 WORDS AND UP ($)
Essay Appraisal	39.95	39.95	39.95	39.95	39.95
Essay Editing	49.95	54.95	59.95	69.95	79.95
Resubmit Edit – No. 1	19.95	19.95	19.95	19.95	19.95
Resubmit Edit – No. 2	24.95	24.95	24.95	24.95	24.95
Sample Essay Service	149.95	159.95	169.95	189.95	199.95

General Comments:

This is another somewhat confusing Web site, partly because it mixes college admission essays with resume writing and scholarship application essays right up front. Focusing on the college admission essay service in isolation; it deals strictly with the evaluation and editing of already written essays at the college entry/undergraduate level. This site is strictly business and offers very little value-added in terms of informational content or support services.

Nevertheless, this site does offer an unusual service called a "Sample Application Essay Writing Service". With this service you send them a copy of your essay question or topic and they draft a "model essay" to address that question or topic. The client is then supposed to use the resulting generic essay as a model for writing their own essay. The idea here being that the model/template essay will be perfect in terms of form and structure and the client just has to adjust the details to fit their personal circumstances and/or approach. This is a novel approach that applies the "real-life template" technique to essay writing.

Bottom Line:

Based on the information presented on the Web site, my best estimate of the minumum cost to complete an *already-drafted* 1,000 word basic college admission essay using this service is $49.95.

For a cost comparison with the other Services, see the Cost Comparison Table in the final chapter.

EssayEdge.com

http://www.essayedge.com/

Service Statement:

(Taken from the Web site of the online Service being reviewed).

EssayEdge.com has been called "the world's premier application essay editing service" by The New York Times Learning Network, and "one of the best essay services on the Internet" by The Washington Post. EssayEdge has helped more applicants write successful application essays than any other company in the world. Our 200+ Harvard-educated editors do not merely offer critiques and proofing; they also provide superior editing, giving you the edge you need in the ultra-competitive college and graduate school application process.

Claim to Fame:

(Taken from the Web site of the online Service being reviewed).

EssayEdge's 200+ Harvard-educated editors have helped more applicants with their admissions essays than any other company in the world. Ninety-four percent of EssayEdge customers are admitted to at least one of their top three schools, and sixty-six percent of EssayEdge customers are admitted to their first-choice school.

EssayEdge employs some of the finest editors in the world; these editors complete a rigorous employment screening process, have professional editing or admissions office experience, and hold graduate, business, law, medical, and undergraduate degrees from Harvard University. On average, EssayEdge rejects 50 applicants for every one person we hire. There simply is no better editing resource than EssayEdge.

According to our 2001 customer poll, on a scale of 1-10, past customers give EssayEdge a 9.1 for quality of editing and an 8.7 for the level of incorporation of EssayEdge edits into the final admissions essay. More importantly, 70 percent of customers submit multiple essays to EssayEdge. Nothing attests to the quality of our editing more than this simple fact! We will satisfy you.

While a few sites on the Internet edit admissions essays, none match EssayEdge's quality editing and excellent prices. While we know that you care more about the quality of the service than the price, EssayEdge is dedicated to maintaining near-zero margins. All our revenues go straight to the editors so that we can afford to hire the best editors in the world; with no overhead, you pay for excellent editing and not our corporate headquarters. While one or two sites may charge $5-10 less than EssayEdge does, most sites charge more.

Subjects Covered:

(These are subject areas <u>specifically</u> covered by the service as per their Web site).

Admission Services:

("Yes" in the "Covered?" column indicates specific mention on their Web site).

COVERED?	SUBJECT AREA	SPECIFIC PRODUCTS/SERVICES
Yes	College (undergraduate)	Admission Essays Personal Statements Scholarship Essays Letter of Recommendation
Yes	Graduate School	Admission Essays Personal Statements Scholarship Essays Letter of Recommendation
Yes	Business School/MBA	Admission Essays Personal Statements Scholarship Essays Letter of Recommendation
Yes	Law School	Admission Essays Personal Statements Scholarship Essays Letter of Recommendation
Yes	Medical School	Admission Essays Personal Statements Scholarship Essays Letter of Recommendation
Yes	Scholarship	Application Essays

Other Related Services:

("Yes" in the "Covered?" column indicates specific mention on their Web site).

COVERED?	PRODUCT OR SERVICE	SPECIFIC PRODUCT/SERVICE
Yes	Advisory Service	Online Forum, Chat Room
Yes	Recommendation Letters	Letter Writing Services.
Yes	Resumes	By An Affiliated Web service.
Yes	Free Samples	Over 100 Free Sample Essays.
Yes	Free Tips	Extensive Free Resource Center.
	Free Newsletter	
Yes	Free Course	Comprehensive Online Course.
Yes	Bookstore	Admissions-Related Collection.

Fees and Charges:

(As published on their Web site July 1, 2002).

SERVICES PROVIDED	0 – 250 WORDS ($)	251 – 900 WORDS ($)	901 – 1,200 WORDS ($)	1,201 – 1,500 WORDS ($)	1,501 – 2,000 WORDS ($)	2001 – 3,000 WORDS ($)	3000 – 4000 WORDS ($)
Opinion Service	24.95	24.95	34.95	44.95	54.95	84.95	114.95
Premium Harvard Edit	24.95	59.95	79.95	99.95	119.95	179.95	239.95
Grand Edit Service	139.95	139.95	159.95	199.95	249.95	349.95	449.95
Comprehensive Edit	199.95	199.95	249.95	299.95	349.95	499.95	649.95
Second Reading Service	39.95	39.95	49.95	59.95	79.95	109.95	139.95
Recommendation Letter	24.95	59.95	79.95	99.95	119.95	179.95	239.95
Scholarship Essay Edit	24.95	59.95	79.95	99.95	119.95	179.95	239.95

General Comments:

This service is clearly one of the "Cadillac" admission essay service on the Net. It offers an extensive range of services, and the Web site is overflowing with free college admission information and resources. It deals with essay writing and support services for all major admission streams: college (undergraduate), graduate, business, law, and medicine. Although EssayEdge is primarily an editing service it does offer some advanced editing services that amount to helping the client develop an essay from scratch.

Of all the services reviewed, this one appears to have the most rigorous approach to the essay review and editing process. The specific process involved for each of the seven (7) services offered is described in detail which should eliminate any confusion as to what one is getting for their money.

I reviewed the EssayEdge.com online Essay Writing Course in detail and it is awesome. It contains between 150 and 200 pages of detailed quality content on how to write your own admission essay starting from a blank page.

Bottom Line:

Based on the information presented on the Web site, my best estimate of the minimum cost to develop a 1,000 word basic college admission essay from scratch using this Service is $249.95.

For a cost comparison with the other Services, see the Cost Comparison Table in the final chapter.

IvyEdge.com

http://www.ivyedge.com/

Service Statement:

(Taken from the Web site of the online Service being reviewed).

Whether you are applying to our nation's most prestigious colleges, law schools, business schools, medical schools, or graduate schools, IvyEdgeConsulting can help.

IvyEdgeConsulting is a different type of Admissions Consulting Company. We utilize the most robust, flexible, and effective admissions strategies for all our clients. Our service succeeds because we combine the experiences of former Admissions Directors with knowledge from students who have succeeded in gaining admissions to the nation's top universities. Our Consultants are bar-none, the best qualified admissions specialists.

The 2002-2003 academic calendar will see close to 90% of prospective students denied admission to the nation's finest universities. This hyper-competitive trend is expected to continue as we progress deeper and deeper into the new millennium. While the vast majority of students applying to these universities have extraordinary standardized test scores, glowing recommendations, phenomenal grade point averages, and numerous extracurricular activities, the admissions essay is often overlooked as a peripheral aspect of the application. Despite the myriad of resources and help pages being offered through the IvyEdge web site, many students still struggle to leave an indelible impression on an admissions committee.

By crafting a refined, engaging, and thought provoking essay, a fair student becomes outstanding, an average student becomes phenomenal, and an exceptional student becomes heroic. Our goal at IvyEdge is to help you create such an essay.

Claim to Fame:

(Taken from the Web site of the online Service being reviewed).
We are a different type of editing service because we set these lofty goals for every single essay we receive. This is what makes us the best, most respected editing service in the world.

Every essay submitted to the IvyEdge Team will receive an in-depth Examination, Critique, and Rewrite.

Remember, having your essay edited by a professional team can give you the edge over the competition. But, you must also do your research. IvyEdge prides itself in our editors' credentials. Our pricing is not rock bottom, while it is not exorbitant either. We will never distribute, promote or use your essay in any way whatsoever, unless you explicitly grant us permission. Our editorial team is always close at hand and ready, willing, and able to answer all your questions.

Subjects Covered:

(These are subject areas *specifically* covered by the service as per their Web site).

Admission Services:

("Yes" in the "Covered?" column indicates specific mention on their Web site).

COVERED?	SUBJECT AREA	SPECIFIC PRODUCTS/SERVICES
Yes	College (undergraduate)	Admission Essays Personal Statements Scholarship Essays Letter of Recommendation
Yes	Graduate School	Admission Essays Personal Statements Scholarship Essays Letter of Recommendation
Yes	Business School/MBA	Admission Essays Personal Statements Scholarship Essays Letter of Recommendation
Yes	Law School	Admission Essays Personal Statements Scholarship Essays Letter of Recommendation
Yes	Medical School	Admission Essays Personal Statements Scholarship Essays Letter of Recommendation
Yes	Scholarship	Application Essays

Other Related Services:

("Yes" in the "Covered?" column indicates <u>specific</u> mention on their Web site).

COVERED?	PRODUCT OR SERVICE	SPECIFIC PRODUCT/SERVICE
Yes	Advisory Service	Extensive Consulting Resources. International Advisors.
Yes	Recommendation Letters	Letter Writing Services.
Yes	Resumes/CVs	Complete Service.
Yes	Free Sample Essays	Excellent Online Collection (rated).
Yes	Free Tips	Online Writing Resource Center. Downloadable Guides.
Yes	Free Newsletter	Insider Secrets From Admission Experts.
Yes	Free Course	Comprehensive Online Course.
	Bookstore	

Fees and Charges:

(As published on their Web site July 1, 2002).

SERVICES PROVIDED (FOR A SINGLE ESSAY/LETTER)	EXAMINATION + CRITIQUE + REVISION (COMPLETED DRAFT PROVIDED) ($)	DEVELOP ESSAY FROM SCRATCH (INCOMPLETE DRAFT PROVIDED ($)
Princeton or Harvard or Yale Service	999.	1,499.
Other Top 30 Program	699.	899.
Second and Third Tier Program	599.	799.
Recommendation Letter	149.	299.

In addition to the above "Single Application Service", IvyEdge also offers a "2-3 Application Service" and a "4-6 Application Service". Rates for these are published on their Web site.

General Comments:

Since I referred to one other Service as the "Cadillac" admission essay service on the Net, well then Ivy Edge has to be the "Mercedes" luxury model. It has a well-designed and extensive Web site, offering a comprehensive range of services. The Web site offers lots of free college admission information and resources including some useful downloads. They handle admission essay writing and support services for all of the major admission streams: college (undergraduate), graduate, business, law, and medicine.

This Service has two overall levels of service for all of its admissions essay work. One level is called "from scratch" although they request at least a rough draft from the client. The other level is called "examination + critique + rewrite" and requires a completed rough draft from the client, up-front.

The Admissions Consulting Service is the most comprehensive (and expensive) that I have seen. There are to overall levels of service here. Consulting with highly-qualified experts ranges from $229 to $329 per hour. Or, you can buy yearlong consulting services packages with these same experts for a fixed price, depending on the program. For example, one-year of consulting advice (including Kaplan Test Prep. Course) costs $13,999 at the undergraduate level and $17,999 for Medical, Law, Graduate, and Business School.

Similar to EssayEdge, this service also provides detailed breakdowns of exactly what it will do for you for each specific level of service offered. So, you get a very good idea of exactly what services you will be receiving for your money, from the outset.

Bottom Line:

Based on the information presented on the Web site, my best estimate of the minimum cost to develop a 1,000 word basic college admission essay from scratch using this Service is $799.

For a cost comparison with the other Services, see the Cost Comparison Table in the final chapter.

COMPARISON OF ADMISSION ESSAY SERVICES

The purpose of the table below is to give you a quick reference guide that directly compares all of the Services reviewed on the basis of cost. I have done this because I understand that cost is the key factor for many students looking for help with college admissions writing.

However, although the cost comparison can be revealing, it alone does not tell the whole story. As I performed my detailed research into these Services, it became clear to me that, in most cases, there is a direct relationship between cost and the quality of service being offered. In general, the more expensive services provide a more in-depth value-added product.

But be careful. There are exceptions to this, especially with straight editing services, so make sure you also do your own research into the details.

COST COMPARISON TABLE

NAME OF ADMISSION ESSAY WRITING SERVICE	EDIT CLIENT ESSAY (1,000 WORDS)	DEVELOP ESSAY FROM SCRATCH (1,000 WORDS)	RECOMMENDATION LETTER (500+ WORDS)
AboutCollegeAdmissions.com	118.90	159.95	n/a
Accepted.com	300.00	575.00	275.00
AdmissionsConsultants.com	190.00	380.00	235.00
AdmissionEssays.com	n/a	285.00	n/a
College-Essays.com	289.00	729.00	n/a
CollegeSuperMall.com	54.95	n/a	n/a
EditMeNow.com	49.95	149.95+	n/a
EssayEdge.com	79.95	249.95	59.95
IvyEdge	599.00	799.00	299.00

Nevertheless, combining the cost information on this table with the service write-ups contained earlier in this report will no doubt help you get "the best bang for your buck", driven of course by your own budget, time, and quality constraints.

I also urge you to do your own review of the Web sites you are considering before you make your final decision. Before doing this, make sure you have narrowed your list of potential Services down to two or three. I say this because when I was researching this guide I spent at least three to four hours on a number of sites. There's a lot of stuff to check out on some of these Web sites.

A small note of caution here. When you do go to review your short-list of potential Service sites, make sure you look below the surface at the Web site. When I was reviewing them I found in a few cases, my initial impression of a particular Service was totally wrong once I did some digging. My detailed reviews of each Service contained in the previous section of this report should help you with that.

And don't be shy about sending the Services on your short list an e-mail question or two about any lingering concerns or questions you may have.

ASSUMPTIONS

Due to the number of different services offered and the numerous ways in which prices are presented by the various online Services, I had to make a number of basic assumptions to ensure that, as much as possible, I was comparing "apples with apples".

Here are the main assumptions that I used in compiling the figures contained in the above cost-comparison table.

- The essay being priced is for the editing or development of a 1,000 word standard college admission essay based on a question or a topic as specified by the college for which application is being made.

- The "Edit Client Essay" column assumes use of the basic editing service provided plus one additional second edit, if not already included in the basic service. For this case, the client would provide an already written essay to the Service and the final product would be an edited and polished essay, ready for submission.

- The "Develop Essay From Scratch" column assumes use of the basic "essay development and writing service" as provided by the Service in question. It assumes that the client would provide the Service with basic personal information, but Not a completed draft essay. The Service agency would work with the client, essentially from either a very preliminary draft outline or a blank piece of paper, in brainstorming, developing, and writing a final edited and polished essay, ready for submission.

- The "Recommendation Letter" column assumes the development of a 500 to 800 word letter of recommendation, essentially from scratch. The client would only provide factual details and perhaps a rough outline of what they "think" the letter should flow like.

- In cases where only hourly rates were provided, I assumed that a complete edit of a 1,000 word client supplied essay would take a minimum of 2.0 hours. I estimated a total of 4.0 hours would be required to develop an essay from scratch and then refine it into final form, ready for submission.

How To Choose

As I mentioned above, the Service you end up choosing will depend on a number of factors relevant to your personal situation such as, budget, time-frame, and quality level required.

In order to use this information to decide on which service to use, I suggest you do the following:

- Refer to the above cost comparison table to get an overall feel for the relative cost of the services involved.

- Based on the information in the table, narrow it down to a short-list of three or four of the services that appear to best match my financial budget constraints.

- Refer to the detailed write-ups on each Service that are contained earlier in this guide to get a better feel for exactly what that service is offering overall in terms of quality and other supplementary services that may be of interest to me. (e.g. advisory service, writing tips, newsletter, bulletin board, etc.).

- Finally, go to the Web sites of whichever Services are left on your list and check them out for yourself. If required, send them e-mails asking for clarification of any outstanding points.

- Once it is narrowed down to one or two Services, send them a final inquiry e-mail asking them to verify your understanding of the services that they will provide, and to confirm your understanding of the approximate cost involved to deal with my specific case. The e-mail would look something like this:

"Hello at EssayWrite.com.

I have drafted the attached 920 word essay on the topic "How I See My Future". As I understand the information on your Web site, it will cost me $79.95 for a first pass by your editors, plus $39.95 for a final review and polishing, if required. Would you please get back to me and confirm my understanding of this.

Thanks very much."

RECOMMENDATION LETTER SERVICES

In the previous section on college admission services I pointed out that a number of those Services also assist clients in drafting recommendation letters that are required to support some college and university program applications.

In addition to those services, there are also a number of online "letter writing services" that can also provide assistance with the various types of letters of recommendation.

Finally, most major resume writing and employment Services provide assistance for writing employment-related recommendation letters.

Accordingly, I have divided these types of sites into three groups that can provide various types of recommendation letters, as follows: employment-related, college admission–related, and general letter-writing services.

(Please note that at the time this list was compiled all of these links were tested and found to be in working order).

EMPLOYMENT-RELATED

The following online Services will draft employment-related recommendation letters for you, for a fee.

A Write Impression… Resume Writing Service
http://www.awriteimpression.com/index.htm

Career Resume Service… Cover letter writing service
http://www.crsresume.com/cover.htm

Monster: A Few Tips on How to Write a Letter of Recommendation.
http://content.monster.com/resume/resources/recommendation/

ResumeEdge.com: Letter of Recommendation Help…
http://www.resumeedge.com/recentgrads/careercenter/recommendations

COLLEGE-RELATED

The following college admission related Services are those that have stated specifically on their Web site that they will assist clients in writing letters of recommendation.

Accepted.com - The Graduate School Letter of Recommendation
http://www.accepted.com/grad/letter_rec.htm

AdmissionsConsultants.com – College admission letters of recommendation.
http://www.admissionsconsultants.com/

EssayEdge: Recommendation Letter Editing
http://www.essayedge.com/college/editing/recletter.shtml

IvyEdge: Admission Essays and Recommendation Letters
http://www.ivyedge.com/Recommendation/recommendation.html

GENERAL LETTER-WRITING SERVICES

The following Web sites offer general letter-writing services, including the writing of recommendation and reference letters.

CrisisBrainstorm.com… Solving your crises... 10 creative solutions at a time
http://www.crisisbrainstorm.com/writing.html

Just The Right Words… Personal and Professional Letter-Writing Service
http://www.jasmincori.com/html/editing_services.htm

LetterExpert.com… Complete Writing Service for Business and Individuals
http://www.letterexpert.com/default.htm

Write101.com… The definitive source for writing on the Web
http://www.write101.com/index.html

WriteExpress.com… Letter Writing and Rhyming Software
http://www.writeexpress.com/cat.html

COMPARISON OF RECOMMENDATION LETTER SERVICES

Please note that this is NOT an exhaustive list of online recommendation letter resources. These are strictly online Services that will draft and/or edit a letter of recommendation for a fee.

The main eBook "Instant Recommendation Letter Kit" contains a complete researched list of online resources related to recommendation letters.

COST COMPARISON TABLE

ONLINE SERVICE	DRAFT A 600 TO 800 WORD RECOMMENDATION LETTER ESTIMATED CHARGE (US$)
Accepted.com	275.
AdmissionsConsultants.com	235.
AWriteImpression.com	100.
CRSresume.com	50.
EssayEdge.com	60.
LetterExpert.com	60.
IvyEdge.com	299.
ResumeEdge.com	60.
Write101.com	50.

Clearly, there is a wide variation in what some of these services will charge you to write a letter of recommendation. Often in life "you get what you pay for, but it is hard to explain what one might get for an additional $200 for one relatively straightforward letter.

The only thing I can suggest here is that you go and take a look at three or four of these Web sites that interest you and find out for yourself how you can get best value for your money. After checking out their online offer you may have to follow-up with an e-mail for further information (see sample below).

Remember to check out their guarantees and whether there could be "additional" charges for second edits, etc. (more on this below).

ASSUMPTIONS

Obtaining reliable cost comparison information from the above-listed sites was a bit tricky. Many of them don't list standard rates for writing recommendation letters. In a number of cases, I had to request a quotation.

The Services listed in the above cost comparison table are the ones that either published a clear rate on their site, or responded to my e-mail with a quotation. If one of the sites listed above is not in the table, you can assume that I was unable to obtain clear information as to how much they would charge.

The case that I used for cost quotation purposes was:

"The drafting of a 1 to 2 page recommendation letter (about 600 to 800 words) with information and a rough draft provided by me."

When dealing with employment-related Services, the recommendation letter is expected to be employment-related. College admission sites are expected to deliver a college admission-related letter of recommendation.

HOW TO CHOOSE

In theory, these online writing services are much more straightforward than the admission essay sites, since they generally deal with straight letter writing. In principle, at least.

Nevertheless, I found that it was easier to get good costing information from the admission essay sites than from most of these letter-writing sites.

Often the pricing information was not listed on the site, and when I made an e-mail request based on the costing criteria given above, a number of them wanted detailed specifications before they would commit themselves. They wouldn't even provide an hourly rate without more details.

Here's what I recommend you do:

- I strongly suggest that you draft the recommendation letter yourself first before hiring one of these services to edit it and fine-tune it. There are so many excellent free resources available on the subject of writing recommendation letters.

- Once you have your "draft" done consult the above Cost Comparison Table to give you a feel for the Services that best meet your budget constraints. From the table, choose a short-list of two or three Services that you are interested in.

- Click through to each of these sites and confirm that you are still interested in dealing with it. Check to see if they have such things as: published prices, guaranteed turnaround times, and unconditional customer satisfaction guarantees, etc.

- Based on the Web site checks, further refine your short-list if necessary and then send each one left on the list a final inquiry e-mail asking them to verify your understanding of the services that they will provide. Also ask them to confirm your understanding of the approximate cost involved to deal with my specific case. The e-mail would look something like this:

    "Hello at LetterWrite.com.

    I have done a rough draft of a 750 word (Insert either: "employment-related" or "college admission") recommendation letter. How much would you charge to review, edit, revise and finalize this letter for submission?

    I was not sure how the pricing information on your Web site would apply to my particular situation.

    Please get back to me ASAP so that I may proceed with this.

    Thanks very much."

NOTES

Printed in the United States
19915LVS00004B/11-28